ORGANIC MANUAL

J. Howard Garrett's

ORGANIC
MANUAL

THE SUMMIT GROUP
FORT WORTH, TEXAS

THE SUMMIT GROUP
1227 West Magnolia, Suite 500, Fort Worth, Texas, 76104

Publisher's Cataloging in Publication

Garrett, Howard, 1947-

    J. Howard Garrett's organic manual / J. Howard Garrett.
    P. cm.

    ISBN 1-56530-082-3

    1. Organic gardening—United States—Handbooks, manuals, etc. I. Title. II. Title: Organic manual.

SB453.58.G37 1993   631.5'84'0973
                        QBI93-448

Jacket design by Cheryl Corbitt and Rishi Seth
Book design by Rishi Seth

Manufactured in the United States of America
First Printing 1989, Revised Printing 1993

FOR LOGAN

CONTENTS

FOREWORD

Modern communications and the increased speed of travel have virtually turned the whole planet into our visible landscape. There are no new frontiers. Most habitable land is being used and abused with the overuse of chemical fertilizers and toxic pesticides.

Thinking people are quickly realizing the pollution this adds to our already overburdened environment. But although information on natural organic farming and vegetable gardening is becoming more and more available, the commercial landscape contractor and the urban dweller with the small bit of nature surrounding his home has up until now been mostly forgotten.

Now, with the *Organic Manual*, Howard Garrett has met this need. The *Organic Manual* combines Howard's immense knowledge of and experience in landscape design and installation with his desire to work in harmony with nature. It's a masterpiece for the home and commercial landscaper.

Howard has a great talent for communicating and the courage it takes to tell the truth. His book not only points out the damage some horticultural chemicals do and shows how they lead down a dead-end road, but gives sensible, earth-friendly alternatives that perform as well as and, in the long run, better than chemicals.

Whenever someone speaks out to try to change the current system, he is sure to draw criticism, and I imagine that Howard Garrett has and will draw his share. But, then, how long can the truth be criticized?

Malcolm Beck

Organic Farmer
Founder of Garden-Ville
Author of *The Garden-Ville Method: Lessons in Nature*

ACKNOWLEDGMENTS

I would like to thank all of the people in the world who have devoted years of their lives to the philosophy of organics. Among them are Sir Alfred Howard, Dr. William Albrecht, J. I. and Robert Rodale, Charles Walters, Dr. Phil Callahan, Arden Anderson, and Malcolm Beck.

Thanks also go to the people who taught me the most about organics and least-toxic pest controls. They include Dr. Dan Clair with the Texas Department of Agriculture, Dr. Paul Syltie with Appropriate Technologies, Dr. Robert Petit with International Humates, Elliott C. Roberts, John Dromgoole, and Malcolm Beck.

I would also like to thank those people who have helped me in their own ways: Judy Garrett, Stan Wetsel, Walter Dahlberg, Barbara Sargent, Carol Harrison, Peggy Grace, Alan Shipley, Sam Frenkil, Bill Neiman, Kim Sinks, Rob Nalley, Derek Little, Kim Anderson, Jim Marshall, Bobby Spence, Charlie Sikes, Jo Harrell, Patti Lancaster, Kevin Starnes, Donna Wilkins, Tracy Flanagan, Odena Brannam, Louise Riotte, Cleve and Kitty Lancaster, Walt Davis, Joe, Peggy and Dalton Maddox, Alan Savory, Martha Sheridan, Bob Bersano, and Jewell and Ruby Garrett.

Thanks should also go to my clients who have been open-minded enough to allow organic techniques and products to be used on their properties. They include Interstate Realty in Memphis, Tennessee; Alcon Laboratories in Fort Worth, Texas; Frito-Lay National Headquarters in Plano, Texas; Johnson & Johnson Medical; Mobil Oil Company; Collin County Community College District; Henry S. Miller Management Corporation; Property Management Systems, Inc.; Coda Energy; and many residential clients.

ABOUT THE AUTHOR

J Howard Garrett is a graduate of Texas Tech University (1969.) He is a landscape architect, publisher, columnist, broadcaster, and organic horticulturist from Pittsburg, Texas. He currently lives in Dallas with his wife Judy and daughter Logan.

In 1988 Howard committed his entire career to the research into, education about, and promotion of organic landscaping, gardening, farming, and basic soil management. He has converted several commercial projects to organic programs. Among them are the corporate facilities of Frito-Lay in Plano, Johnson and Johnson in Arlington, and Mobil Oil in Dallas. The 100-acre campus of Collin County Community College was the first of his large-scale commercial successes.

Thousands of homeowners have now switched to his organic program. Not only are these properties doing well, but they are in better shape than they ever were on synthetic-chemical programs. The public has responded so positively to organics that grass-roots pressure has forced Texas A&M to initiate their

Earth Kind program, and large chain nurseries have all dedicated space in their stores to organic programs.

Apart from his organic work, he has designed and consulted on landscaping projects in all the major cities in Texas as well as in several other parts of the country. Those projects include Frito-Lay National Headquarters in Plano; Alcon Laboratories, American Airlines Headquarters, and The Golf Club at Fossil Creek, all in Fort Worth; Spring Creek Campus of Collin County Community College in Plano; San Antonio Hyatt Resort; and residential gardens.

Currently, he is president of Coda Environmental and Restoration and owner of Lantana Publishing Company. He is host of the WBAP Gardening Show *The Natural Way* on Sundays and columnist for *The Dallas Morning News* "The Natural Way" in Friday's House and Garden section.

Howard has written four books: *Plants of the Metroplex, Howard Garrett's Texas Organic Gardening, Landscape Design...Texas Style*, and *J. Howard Garrett's Organic Manual*.

1

INTRODUCTION

INTRODUCTION

Organics is the thoughtful and sensitive use of techniques and products that not only sustain but improve soil health and the environment in general.

Organic programs are really quite simple. It just requires understanding that nature cannot be divided into parts. Nothing can be added or taken away without causing a chain reaction. Creation, birth, death, decay, and rebirth are all elements in the chain of life and are all connected.

The practice of growing plants using organic techniques has been used for as long as man has tilled the earth. Only since World War II has the world of agriculture and horticulture been changed by the introduction of synthetic fertilizers and pesticides. The proliferation of these chemicals temporarily increased the yield of many crops, including ornamentals, but also increased the long-term cost of production, caused pollution of our drinking water, changed the soil structure, accelerated erosion, and jarred the entire ecosystem. The earth's fertile land has been depleted, and overall production has decreased due to a dramatic reduction of the soil's health.

Reasons for the continued use of synthetic products include a lack of understanding of how organic techniques work and the fear that, if chemicals are discontinued, plants won't grow well and will be devoured by insects and disease. The amount of money spent on chemical advertising and chemical research at major universities is of no small consequence either. Many people don't know that organic products work effectively and economically and are easy and fun to use. On the other hand, most folks don't realize how dangerous and damaging harsh pesticides and synthetic fertilizers are, not only to themselves, but to the health of the planet.

CHEMICALS VS. ORGANICS

It's not a chemical vs. organics question. Everything in the world is chemical. Even air and water are composed of chemicals such as hydrogen, oxygen, nitrogen, and carbon.

The words "chemical" and "organic"

are equally misused and misunderstood. For example, there are products acceptable for use in an organic program that have low toxicity but are not truly organic, and some organic products are extremely dangerous and not acceptable in a wise organic program. Likewise, not all chemical products are severely toxic. Confused?

The point is that the two words, "chemical" and "organic," have become the passwords for the two philosophies. "Chemical" represents the traditional approach of force-feeding the plants using synthetic fertilizers and trying to control nature using synthetic pesticides, while "organic" represents the approach of working with nature to improve soil health and using the least toxic and most environmentally sensitive products available.

It's a big misconception that organic methods are simply safer ways to kill pests. The basis of organics is an overall philosophy of life more than a simple decision about which kinds of garden products to use. The organic philosophy relates to the ability to see and understand nature's systems and work within those systems. The chemical philosophy teaches that man and his products can control nature. But nature can't be controlled—it's really futile to even try. Many farmers have come to see that, and they are now realizing that we must stop taking the life out of the soil and the land out of production. The landscaping industry is also moving very quickly toward the organic philosophy, primarily because of the tremendous public demand for safer and more envi-

ronmentally sensitive techniques and products.

However, chemicals are not all bad. For example, some of the best tools in the organic gardener's arsenal include synthetic products like *Logic* fire ant control, *Precor*, *Altocid*, and other pest-control products. They work by regulating the growth of insects rather than by killing the pests. These products have very low toxicity to beneficial insects, pets, man, and the environment.

On the other hand, some of the best tools of the organic gardener are extremely toxic materials. For example, Bt and Bti are very toxic, natural, biological products. Fortunately, they are specific to the targeted pests—caterpillars and mosquitoes—and they don't hurt beneficial insects, pets, man, or the environment.

Another difference in philosophy relates to fertilization. Traditional "chemical" proponents say that plants must be fertilized with a 3-1-2 or 4-1-2 ratio fertilizer 4 times a year. The organic philosophy contends that the soil should be fed and balanced and that plants don't need to be force-fed. Balancing the soil is not discussed very often, if ever, in the traditional chemical programs.

The balance of chemistry, physics, and biology is the key. Remember that everything is chemical. If the chemistry of the soil is balanced, the physical properties will be correct, the pH will be between 6.2 and 6.5, and the biology will also be in the proper proportions. Calcium should represent approximately 60-70% of the available chemical nutrients, magnesium 10-20%, potassium 2-5%, and sodium .5-3%, and all the trace elements should be in their proper relative proportions.

Another advantage of balanced soil chemistry is that fertilizer inputs can be greatly reduced. In fact, once the soil is balanced properly, the maintenance of plants can be done primarily with mulches, organic matter, foliar feeding, and an occasional fine tuning of the balance of the minerals of the soil.

Therefore, if the chemicals in the soil are balanced (those chemicals that *should* be there, that is) everything else will fall in line. A chemically balanced soil will have proper tilth, positive drainage, and the correct populations of living organisms—if you stop killing them with the quick-fix lawn-care poisons. The end result is healthy plants, animals, and people.

So you see—chemicals aren't so bad, and "organics" is just the rallying cry.

REVERSING THE CHEMICAL ADDICTION

There are two major soil pollutants—fertilizers and pesticides. Synthetic chemical fertilizers are the most common chemicals used in farming, gardening, and landscaping. These man-made fertilizers are merely soluble-salt compounds, usually found in granulated form, and relatively inexpensive. Synthetic fertilizers provide nothing to benefit the soil; in fact, they leave considerable amounts of salt residue and other contamination.

Since the plants will not absorb large quantities of salt, continued use of salt-based fertilizers can lead to loss of plant quality, loss of productivity, and, in extreme cases, phytotoxicity (poisoning of the plants). Another point to note is that these fertilizers will repel and kill beneficial soil microorganisms and earthworms. Synthetic fertilizers are harsh and interfere with the natural chemical, physical, and biological systems in the soil.

High levels of nitrates, which are created by synthetic-nitrogen fertilizers, are carcinogenic and frequently show up in our drinking water. Because of the overuse of high-nitrogen fertilizers and the plant's inability to use large amounts of nitrogen, the excess is simply leached or washed away and ends up ultimately in our streams, lakes, and aquifers.

Pesticides are the second most common chemicals applied to plants and soil. Pesticides include insecticides, fungicides, herbicides, and any other poisons used to kill plants or animals. Excess pesticides destroy the microscopic living organisms of the soil. Pesticides will also affect plant growth, and, when absorbed by the plant, begin passing through the food chain. All living organisms are affected—microorganisms, insects, animals, and man. It should also be noted that, if used too often at excessive rates, pesticides can virtually sterilize the soil if leaching does not occur.

When pesticides *are* leached out, they end up in streams or ground water, available to enter the food chain this way. Huge amounts of toxic chemicals are used on home lawns and agricultural crops, making the use of chemicals a serious problem in urban as well as rural areas. Insects and diseases get blamed for the use of these toxins, but they are not the problem, only the symptom of the problem. The real problem is poor soil health, and that problem is increased with each application of toxic chemicals. Chemical programs create a drug dependency and, unfortunately, they control mainstream agriculture and horticulture.

The damage to our soil's health can be reversed by returning it to a natural balance. Those of us in the landscape industry and the agriculture industry must take the lead, but homeowners must also get involved in reducing and ultimately eliminating the toxic chemicals we dump into our environment. Besides being dangerous, they aren't necessary.

Thirty-five years ago, J. I. and Robert Rodale began the organic movement in the United States using the studies and writings of Sir Albert Howard of England and Dr. William A. Albrecht of the University of Missouri. The Rodales convinced many home gardeners and some farmers to add humus to the soil through organic matter and minerals through natural mineral powders to improve the health and nutrition of food crops. The idea was quite simple: healthy soil produces healthy plants; healthy plants produce healthy animals and humans. It's possible that the simplicity has been one of the major roadblocks. How could something so simple work? A more powerful obstacle has been the concern, "How are we going to make money?"

The purpose of this book is to explain how organic techniques work and what products are best to use in a complete, 100% organic program. The goal is to convince you to use organic programs on farm and ranch and landscaping and greenhouse operations.

You will learn that organic land management offers reduced long-term costs and liabilities and creates and maintains a safe, healthy environment for all concerned.

Food crops grown organically are a critical ingredient in eliminating disease. The elimination of pesticide residue is important, but not the most important issue. Health is the primary issue, and real health comes from eating food containing a proper balance of mineral nutrients and energy. Healthy food can only come from healthy soil.

2

HEALTHY SOILS

HEALTHY SOILS

Soil and dirt are two very different things. Dirt is an inert planting medium that holds up plants. Soil is a wonderfully dynamic, ever-changing, complex, living system of life, energy, and minerals. Soil, like all parts of the environment, is fragile. It is also hard to repair once damaged. Unfortunately, most conventional landscape and agriculture procedures have damaged and are continuing to damage the soil. The key is to stop the damage by starting to use management techniques, soil amendments, fertilizers, and pest-control products that benefit soil health.

Soil, along with water, air, and sunlight, is one of the basic building blocks of life on earth.

For years the soil has been abused. Man has for so long taken from the land without giving back that the soil in much of the world has died and become desert-like where it once was thriving and productive. Deserts aren't just sand dunes. Dead lakes and rivers are deserts. Chemically abused farms and chemically treated urban lawns have become deserts. The definition of "desert" is land that has lost its biological diversity. We can reverse the trend by preserving healthy soil and rebuilding dead and unbalanced soil. We must reestablish biodiversity. A mix of microbes, insects, snakes, toads, lizards, birds, mammals, annuals, perennials, trees, grasses, herbs, and wildflowers must be present. Large masses of one plant type or monocultures must be eliminated. Nature abhors a straight line and nature abhors a monoculture. Forests that have been replanted after clear cutting are "deserts." Desertification of the world must end or the world will end—earlier than scheduled!

*Healthy soil is a dynamic living community
of air, water, organic matter, minerals and
living organisims.*

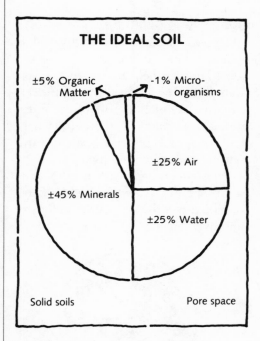

THE IDEAL SOIL

±5% Organic Matter — -1% Micro-organisms

±25% Air

±45% Minerals

±25% Water

Solid soils · Pore space

Healthy soil is a balance of physics, chemistry, and biology. It is a mixture of minerals, organic matter, living organisms, water, and air. It contains 25% air, 25% water, 45% minerals, 5% humus, and living organisms. Healthy soil is aerated, rich in organic matter, and alive with insects, earthworms, and microscopic plants and animals. It is well-drained, sweet smelling, moist, and rich in a wide variety of minerals and nutrients. It is also highly energized.

ORGANIC MATTER

Organic matter is anything that was once living. Every living thing dies, and everything that dies, rots. All organic matter biodegrades. It's during that process that microorganisms reduce once-living matter into basic elements of fertility.

However, the constant tilling of the soil, growth of plants, and removal of organic matter without replenishment will ultimately reduce the soil to an inorganic state, rendering it useless for healthy plant growth.

When organic matter such as leaves break down, becoming dark brown and crumbly, the resulting product is humus. Humus is soft, crumbly, amorphous, and sweet smelling. It holds and slowly releases minerals and nutrients to the plants.

Maintaining a constant supply of organic matter is essential to start and continue an organic program. Good sources of organic matter for the soil include composted materials, green cover crops, vegetable and animal waste, root exudates, and the dead bodies of insects and microorganisms.

SOIL MICROORGANISMS

You don't hear much about soil microorganisms from the conventional horticulturists and farmers. Microorganisms are microscopic plants and animals living in the soil. They are the "life" in the soil. They include bacteria, fungi, actinomycetes, algae, protozoa, yeast, germs, ground pearls, and nematodes. There are about 50 billion microbes in 1 tablespoon of soil. There are approximately 900,000,-000,000 (nine hundred billion) microorganisms per pound of healthy soil.

To give you a clear idea of the population of these vital microbes, the estimated numbers of common organisms found in each gram of reasonably healthy agricultural soils are as follows:

Bacteria	3,000,000	to	500,000,000
Actinomycetes	1,000,000	"	20,000,000
Fungi	5,000	"	1,000,000
Yeast	1,000	"	1,000,000
Protozoa	1,000	"	500,000
Algae	1,000	"	500,000
Nematodes	10	"	5,000

Note: 1 gram is the approximate weight of a paper clip.

The microorganisms' primary job is to break down organic matter—first into humus, then humic acid, and ultimately into basic elements. This process is known as mineralization. Microbes must have a constant supply of organic matter or they will be reduced in population and weaken the soil. Certain microorganisms also have the ability to fix nitrogen from the air, which is approximately 80% nitrogen. Unhealthy soil will not support plant growth without artificial foods and stimulants. Healthy soils produce food through microbial feeding. Microbes are constantly being born and are constantly dying. It's okay for microorganisms to die because that is the natural process. The dead bodies of microorganisms are actually an important source of organic matter in healthy soil.

Soil moisture is important to the health of microorganisms. Beneficial microbes thrive in soil that is neither

dry nor soggy but about as wet as a squeezed-out sponge. Healthy soil is easier to keep at the proper moisture level and can help to save money on water bills. In fact, healthy organic soil can save as much as 50% of the water normally used for irrigation of soil where large quantities of harsh pesticides and synthetic fertilizers are used.

Most microorganisms need a constant supply of oxygen. Therefore, aeration of unhealthy soil is critical for soil improvement.

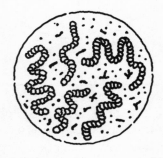

ALGAE: Algae account for the majority of the photosynthetic microflora of the soil. They thrive primarily on or near the soil surface where light and moisture are adequate, although some algae can always be found in the subsoil. Algae produce organic matter by taking carbon dioxide from the air and energy from sunlight to create new cells. Fungi and bacteria can reduce the net amount of organic matter, but algae increase the volume. They are much less numerous than bacteria, fungi, and actinomycetes but are extremely important. Blue-green algae (also called cyanobacteria) are able to fix or grab nitrogen directly from the air in the soil.

NEMATODES: Nematodes are probably the most numerous multicellular creatures on earth. They are active, tubular, microscopic animals living on moist surfaces or in liquid environments like the films of water in the soil. Destructive and beneficial nematodes exist in all soils. Some create knots on roots and some enter through lesions to feed on roots. Some species of beneficial nematodes are being used to control termites, grubworms, and other pests.

ACTINOMYCETES: Actinomycetes generally thrive in well-aerated, neutral to alkaline soils. They are less active in acid or waterlogged soils but are extremely important to the decay of organic matter in dry regions. They are visible as the white, fungus-like threads on decaying organic matter. The earthy smell of newly plowed soil or the forest floor is compliments of actinomycetes. They are a higher form of bacteria and similar to fungi and molds. Actinomycetes are very important in the formation of humus. Actinomycetes may work near the surface or many feet below the ground. While decomposing animal and vegetable matter, actinomycetes liberate carbon, nitrogen, and ammonia, making mineral nutrients available for higher plants.

BACTERIA: Bacteria thrive under a wide variety of conditions from acid to alkaline and from aerobic (with free oxygen) to anaerobic (lack of free oxygen) conditions. Bacteria help in the decay of organic matter, encourage organic and inorganic chemical reactions that have a profound effect on plant growth, and fix nitrogen from the air in the soil. Most bacteria are found in the top one foot or so of soil.

PROTOZOA: Protozoa are the simplest form of animals. They are single-celled and microscopic in size. They obtain their food from organic matter. Protozoa serve to regulate the size of the bacterial community.

FUNGI: Fungi are multicelled and filamentous or single-celled, primitive plants. They lack chlorophyll and therefore lack the ability to make their own carbohydrates. Fungi thrive mainly in well-drained, neutral to acidic, oxygenated soils. Mycorrhizal fungi help the development of healthy root systems by growing on roots and effectively enlarging the length and surface area of roots. Fungi are visible as white, cobweb-like threads that actually enter the cells of the root hairs.

SOIL MACROORGANISMS

Healthy soil is not only full of billions of microorganisms, but it also contains many macroorganisms. These organisms can be seen with the naked eye. They range from tiny mites to large rodents and all have a specific function or purpose in the soil. The most famous and most helpful macroorganism is the earthworm. Earthworms till and aerate the soil, increase drainage, stimulate microbiotic activity, and increase soil fertility. It's impossible to have too many earthworms.

Macroorganisms can be divided into three major subgroups: herbivores, detritivores, and carnivores, although some may fall into more than one subgroup. Herbivores feed on living plants, detritivores feed on dead and decaying plant tissues, and carnivores feed on other living organisms (both micro and macroorganisms). Herbivores (plant eaters) include snails, slugs, insect larvae, termites, beetle larvae, woodchucks, mice, and grubs. Detritivores (decaying matter eaters) include mites, snails, beetles, millipedes, woodlice, springtails, earthworms, worms, spiders, scorpions, centipedes, earwigs, crickets, termites, slugs, and ants. Carnivores (animal eaters) include mites, springtails, enchytraeds, centipedes, snails, slugs, flies, moles, ants, spiders, centipedes, scorpions, and beetles.

Macroorganisms loosen the soil by burrowing and digging, help decompose plant tissue for use by microorganisms, and help to create beneficial compounds that plants can utilize. For example, an earthworm will bring valuable minerals from deep in the soil up to the surface as it burrows up and down. These minerals can be used by the plant, and the burrowing helps oxygen permeate to the plant's roots. Earthworms also take organic matter from the surface and pull it down into the soil.

While some macroorganisms can be considered harmful or destructive to plant roots, their presence may also be valuable to the health of the soil. They may be an important food source for other organisms. The principles of organics teach that helping all pieces of nature work in harmony is essential. If we try to kill all the macroorganisms that are detrimental, we will certainly kill the beneficial ones as well. Balance in a healthy soil is the goal. When the balance is disrupted, the symptoms of insects and diseases occur.

MINERALS

The soil's most plentiful major component is mineral matter. In the top 6" of healthy soil, the mineral portion will be approximately 45%. The mineral composition is the principal determinant of the soil's property. Minerals occur as a result of the physical or chemical action of the parent rock near the surface of the soil. There are 92 naturally occurring mineral elements.

Minerals are responsible for the growth of a plant's cells. Plants depend on 3 essential nutrients derived from carbon dioxide and water: carbon, hydrogen, and oxygen. Plants also depend on 13 essential nutrients derived from the minerals in the soil as inorganic salts—iron, potassium, calcium, magnesium, nitrogen, phosphorous, sulfur, manganese, chlorine, boron, zinc, copper, and molybdenum. The other 70 or so trace minerals are not fully understood but are important to the soil, to plants, and to nature's whole.

But organic fertilizers do not have very high amounts of nitrogen, phosphorous, and potassium. Aren't these amounts important? When fertilizing or adding mineral nutrients, it's important to think about balance. Healthy soils and plants have a balance of ele-

ments and ingredients. A proper fertilization program will help keep that balance intact. That's why it's important to avoid an overkill of the well-known elements nitrogen, phosphorous, and potassium.

Here's a good example. The following are the percentages of various elements in whole plants:

Oxygen	45 percent
Carbon	44 percent
Hydrogen	6 percent
Nitrogen	2 percent
Potassium	1.1 percent
Phosphorous	0.4 percent
Sulfur	0.5 percent
Calcium	0.6 percent
Magnesium	0.3 percent

Note the relatively low percentages of nitrogen, phosphorous, and potassium and the high percentages of oxygen, carbon, and hydrogen.

When buying fertilizer, remember how relatively unimportant nitrogen, phosphorous, and potassium are. They are important but not as important as balance. Think in terms of providing to the soil those products and elements that will help maintain the natural balance. If the soil is in a healthy, balanced condition (which includes organic matter and air), nitrogen, potassium, and phosphorous will be produced naturally by the feeding of microorganisms and relatively little will need to be added.

MINERAL NUTRIENTS

OXYGEN: is an often overlooked element. Adding oxygen to most soils can cause an immediate healthy response in plants, much the same effect as using high-nitrogen fertilizer. Oxygen can be added to the soil by mechanical means such as aerifying or tilling, but it also can be added by using organic fertilizers and soil conditioners. Healthy plants, with their extensive root systems, also can be very beneficial for introducing oxygen into the all-important top 12" of soil.

NITROGEN: is an essential constituent of proteins and vital to plant health. However, excessive nitrogen can cause an imbalance in plant metabolism, which can adversely affect plant growth, fruiting, and storage life.

Nitrogen is an ingredient of proteins and distinguishes them from carbohydrates. The amount of nitrogen in a given material is determined by dividing the percent of protein by 6.25— i.e., cottonseed meal is 60% protein divided by 6.25 equals 10% nitrogen. Unlike other nutrients, it does not originate from the soil but from the air. Nitrogen enters the soil through rain or by being fixed by organisms associated with legumes such as clover, peas, beans, or alfalfa. Some organisms such as blue-green algae can fix nitrogen without an association with plants. The air is approximately 80% nitrogen. Lack of vigor and yellowing of the oldest leaves are signs of nitrogen deficiency.

PHOSPHATE: is the soil's catalyst. Its most important function is to help transfer the energy in the plant from one point to another. Adequate phosphorous is needed for color and vitality of the plant at bloom time and at maturity. It also increases seed and flower size. Soils must have high levels of phosphates so that enough sugars are formed in the plants. Sources include: colloidal phosphate, superphosphate, rock phosphate, and phosphoric acid. Deficiency characteristics are weak flower and fruit production.

CARBON: is essential for the availability of nitrogen and phosphate and is an important food source for microorganisms. Between 45 and 56% of a plant's compounds contain carbon. Carbon is also a significant source of soil and plant energy. Sources of carbon include compost, manures, humates, and coal.

CALCIUM: is the king of the nutrients. It is the most critical in low humus soils. Calcium is needed to feed the microbes and affect the permeability of plant cell walls and the thickness of stems. Sources include: lime (calcitic limestone or calcium carbonate), gypsum, marl, and dolomitic lime (which is the worst choice because of magnesium). Deficiency characteristics include die-back of growth tips in tops and roots and increased susceptibility to disease.

HYDROGEN: is a nonmetallic element that is the simplest and lightest of all and is the third most plentiful element in plants. It is flammable and the most abundant element in the universe. Hydrogen combines with oxygen to form water (H_2O) and hydrogen peroxide (H_2O_2).

MAGNESIUM: has more effect on pH than calcium does. It is important for photosynthesis and helps hold the soil together. Magnesium aids in phosphate metabolism. Plants will show a deficiency if there is too much or too little magnesium. Deficiency will cause thin leaves and yellowing between veins from the bottom of the plant up. Sources include: Sul-Po-Mag, Epsom salts (magnesium sulfate), magnesium oxide, and compost.

POTASSIUM: or potash is a metabolic regulator and is essential to the balance between leaf and root growth and necessary for winter and summer hardiness. This element exists in ample quantities in many soils but is often tied up due to mineral imbalance. Sources include: granite, greensand, potassium sulfate, Sul-Po-Mag, molasses, and compost. Deficiency characteristics include early winter-kill, poor survival of perennials, and increased susceptibility to disease.

SULFUR: called secondary, is actually a major element. Like nitrogen, a deficiency causes yellow leaves but a nitrogen deficiency affects the older leaves first. Sulfur deficiency turns the newest leaves yellow. Sulfur is the easiest leached of all minerals. Sulfur improves the taste of food, increases protein content, and promotes seed production. Sources include compost, molasses, sulfates, elemental sulfur, gypsum, and compost.

CHLORIDE: is needed in balanced soils, although excessive amounts can be a great problem in the soil. Sources include city-treated water and compost.

SODIUM: is most important in its rela-tionship with potassium. The available potassium must be higher than the available sodium. Adequate amounts of sodium help to prevent diseases. Sources include most manures, baking soda, and compost.

BORON: is important for nitrogen efficiency and disease resistance and lets you use less nitrogen. Deficiencies show up as purple leaves, reduced sugar content, bitter taste, cracks in root crops, and corkiness. Boron exists in all cell membranes and is important for nitrogen fixation. Boron works closely with calcium and contributes more than any other micronutrient to the quality of produce. Other deficiency symptoms: tip growth dies, buds turn light green, roots brown in the center, flowers don't form. Boron is also important for disease resistance. Sources include Solubor, Borax, and compost.

IRON: is an essential element for photosynthesis and for the green color in plants. Deficiency shows up as yellow on youngest leaves from top to bottom (veins, margins, and tips stay green). Iron is often tied up in calcareous soils. Sources include copperas (ferrous sulfate), chelated iron, and several organic fertilizers.

MANGANESE: deficiency shows up as white tissue between the veins. Plants will be dwarfed and leaves will have dead spots. If sodium plus potassium equals 10% or more of the available nutrients, no manganese will get to the plant. Sources include manganese sulfates, chelates, and compost.

COPPER: is an important micronutrient for disease resistance. Most soils are deficient in copper. One reason is that too much nitrogen ties up copper. Most common sources are copper sulfate and compost.

ZINC: availability requires a well-aerated soil and is important for the sweet taste in vegetables and fruit. Deficiency shows in leaves with dead areas, poor bud formation, and small terminal leaves. Weed pressure is greater when zinc is deficient. Sources include kelp meal, liquid seaweed, zinc sulfate, and compost.

MOLYBDENUM: is important in natural nitrogen fixation but usually unavailable in acid soils. Healthy plants will usually have between .01 and 10 ppm. Other than being important for the health of certain microbes, there is much mystery about the importance of molybdenum. Sources include most all organic fertilizers and compost.

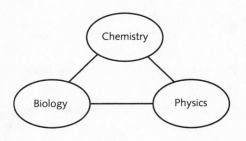

The health, balance, and productivity of the soil depends on three basic pieces being in place: chemistry, biology, and physics. They are all three dependent upon each other. The soil's chemistry must be balanced for the physics and biology to be correct. The living portion of the soil must be healthy for the tilth and drainage to work properly, and the physical properties of the soil must be correct for the living organisms to thrive. Nature will balance the soil for you over time if a few basic ingredients are added and maintained: organic matter, air, and moisture.

HOW PLANTS GROW

The sunlight is the source of all energy. Green leaves are the instruments for gathering in the sunlight. Sunlight energy and the gas called carbon dioxide (CO_2) enter the foliage of plants to combine with water and chlorophyll to form sugars, proteins, fats, and carbohydrates, the food stuff of plants. This process is known as *photosynthesis*. This naturally created food is transferred from the foliage through the stems and limbs down through the trunk into the roots and out into the soil in the form of exudates. Exudates in the form of dead cells and gel-like materials leave the roots through the root hairs and enter the rhizosphere.

The rhizosphere is the soil area that is immediately adjacent to the roots. It is the location of the heaviest concentration of microbiotic activity. Some of the beneficial soil microorganisms include: mycorrhizal fungi, nitrogen-fixing bacteria, yeasts, algae, cyanobacteria, actinomycetes, protozoa, mites, and other small animals and beneficial nematodes. Here the roots and soil are working together to produce and release nutrients to feed the plant.

Microorganisms of all sorts feed on the soil's energy-rich substances, releasing a vast array of minerals, vitamins, antibiotics, regulators, enzymes, and other compounds that can be absorbed into the roots and taken back into the plant to produce strong growth and increased pest and disease resistance. Roots take up nutrients from the soil and pass them up into the plant, causing stem and leaf top growth.

Whether the plant is a bluebonnet, bur oak, or blue grass, the process is the same. This natural process only works at its full potential and efficiency if the soil is healthy.

HOW TO START AN ORGANIC PROGRAM

Now that many homeowners and businesses have successfully converted to organic programs, the interest and enthusiasm is spreading rapidly. My most often-asked question is, "How do I get started?"

Remember that organic agriculture, gardening, and landscaping all have the same basic philosophy of working with nature's systems to maintain the soil, food crops, and ornamental plants without synthetic fertilizers or harsh, chemical pesticides.

Organic fertilizers stimulate soil microorganisms and earthworms, provide humus, and help to aerate the soil. They also provide major nutrients—nitrogen, phosphorous, and potash, as well as secondary nutrients— calcium, sulfur, and magnesium, and trace elements such as copper, zinc, boron, manganese, and molybdenum. In addition, organic techniques help to save water by allowing soils to drain well while maintaining proper moisture levels for longer periods of time.

Organic programs work with nature's laws and systems rather than try to fight and control nature as chemical programs do.

I'm reluctant to say it's easy because anything new seems hard at first, especially when a completely new thought process is required. Conventional hor-

ticulture and ag programs are based on force-feeding plants and killing pests. Organic programs are based on encouraging health and working within nature's laws to help her control life the natural way.

If you are ready to start your organic program, here's how it works.

1 **AERATE THE SOIL:** Use power machinery or hand tools to punch holes in the soil. Oxygen is usually the most limiting factor in unhealthy soils. This is a critical step in all soils except those that are sandy and well drained.

2 **MOW AT A HIGHER SETTING:** Raise the mowing height to at least 2^1/$_2$". Leave the clippings on the ground. Grass clippings are an important source of organic matter and contain needed nutrients. Excess clippings after heavy rains or missed mowings can be put in the compost pile.

3 **DO NOT SCALP THE LAWN:** Let me repeat—*do not* scalp the lawn. Not only is there no benefit from this who-knows-how-it-started procedure, but scalping encourages weeds by exposing bare soil to sunlight, which causes crabgrass and other annual weeds to germinate. Plus, the organic matter should be left on the ground to feed the microorganisms.

4 **STOP USING HERBICIDES:** Preemergents are sprout killers that only help with annual weeds such as crabgrass and grass burs, both of which can be eliminated with proper culture. Perennial weeds can be spot-killed with vinegar but remember that healthy soil and lawn grasses will choke out most noxious weeds. Plus, remember that some so-called weeds are not noxious. I actually

encourage clover, wildflowers, and herbs in the lawn.

5 **START A COMPOST PILE:** All vegetative matter should go into the pile—never send any vegetative waste to the dump. Everything that's alive dies and everything that dies rots; therefore, you can compost anything that was once alive. Keep the pile moist and turn it at least monthly. Finished compost can be tilled into the soil and partially finished compost (raw material can still be identified) is an excellent top-dressing mulch. Containers are only for convenience and tarp coverings are not needed. Compost piles work in sun or shade, and, if they are kept aerated, they don't stink. Do not use synthetic or greasy ingredients.

6 **START FERTILIZING WITH ORGANIC FERTILIZER:** Fertilize in early spring and again in early to midsummer. Timing is not critical since we are feeding the soil instead of the plants. The usual rate is about 20 lbs. per 1,000 sq. ft. Acceptable organic fertilizers include cottonseed meal, alfalfa meal, soybean meal, fish meal, or manufactured organic fertilizers such as GreenSense, Earth Safe, Maestro-Gro, Sustane, Ringer, Tomas, or other 100% organic fertilizers.

7 **USE SPECIAL FERTILIZERS ON FLOWERS:** Add earthworm castings at 10 lbs./1,000 sq. ft. and bat guano at 10 lbs. to all flowering plants once per season or at each color change. Fish meal is another good choice.

8 **MULCH ALL BARE SOIL:** I know you may get tired of hearing me say this, but it's the most important single step in the organic program. Almost any organic matter can be used as a mulch, but the best choices are shredded native wood chips and shredded hardwood bark for ornamentals and alfalfa hay for vegetables. The worst choice is peat moss. The second worse choice is fine-textured pine bark or other small-particled material.

9 **SPRAY ALL PLANTS:** with a mixture of fish emulsion and liquid seaweed. If you're like my wife and get nauseated at the smell of fish emulsion, use Bioform, which is a product that contains fish emulsion, seaweed, and molasses. Yes, molasses is an excellent ingredient. It not only provides an excellent food source for microorganisms, it virtually eliminates the fish emulsion odor.

10 **RELEASE BENEFICIAL INSECTS:** Beneficial bugs should be released every two weeks during the growing season until healthy naturalized populations exist. The best choices for general control are ladybugs, green lacewings, praying mantids, and various wasps.

11 **DO NOT SPRAY CHEMICAL PESTICIDES:** or you will blow the money you just spent on step 10.

12 **SPRAY FOR PEST CONTROL WITH ORGANIC PESTICIDES BUT ONLY AS A LAST RESORT:** Strong water blasts will control many pests, including aphids and red spider mites. Garlic/pepper tea is an excellent and healthy preventative.

13 **ENCOURAGE BIODIVERSITY:** Plant a variety of plant materials and use natives and well-adapted introductions. Using exotic plants that are hard to maintain violates the organic principles. Don't forget to feed the birds and encourage other friends such as bats, lizards, toads, and insects.

Please remember that you are dealing with living soil, living plants, and other living creatures. Nature is dynamic and always changing. No program is the best for everyone, so start out with my program and then fine-tune it into your own. No single organic program is perfect—except for nature's own.

BUILDING A HEALTHY SOIL

Building a healthy soil is done by putting the basic elements in place and letting Mother Nature do the rest. Most unhealthy soils lack air and humus, have a weak population of microorganisms, and are chemically unbalanced. All these things are related, and improving any one of them indirectly improves the others.

The first step in major soil improvement is to aerate the ground. Cultivated and pasture land can be ripped or chisel plowed, and turf areas should be mechanically aerated. Ornamental beds should be aerated with a turning fork or hand aerator.

The next step is have the soil tested. Soil samples may be collected any time. However, *if no samples have been taken on an area within the last two years, the best time to sample is as soon as possible*. Soil testing should be done every year ideally and at the same time of year.

STEPS TO SOIL TESTING

1 **PREPARE A MAP OF THE AREAS TO BE TESTED:** A good map makes your sampling repeatable from year to year and is useful at the time of fertilization. Divide the landscape, field, or pasture into areas where the soil has the same color, slope, surface, texture, internal drainage, and past history of erosion. Each area should have the same plant type (i.e., beds, turf, etc.). Assign each of the areas sampled a letter. For example, Area #1 could have three areas: A—the high ground, B—the sloping ground, and C—the low, level ground. The numbers written on the sample bags would be 1A, 1B, and 1C. As a general rule, any area that is different in slope, texture, color, etc. and large enough to be fertilized separately should also be sampled separately.

2 **COLLECT THE SAMPLE:** Using a soil probe or trowel, push the probe down to plow depth or $6^{1}/_{2}$–7". (4" for no-till, pastures, and lawns.) Remove any grass or thatch on top and put the rest of the probing into a soil sample bag or plastic container. Ziploc bags are fine—as long as they have *never* been used. Do not use paper sacks from the grocery store, bread wrappers, etc. due to possible contamination. Avoid using previously used buckets. Probe the soil every 50 to 100 paces, always taking a minimum of 5 probes per composite sample for small areas, and one probe for every one or two acres from larger areas. Only a small amount of soil is necessary for analysis.

3 **LABEL THE BAGS:** Indicate name and area letters on the sample bag. Make sure the labeling on the bag matches the number of the area on the map it is to represent. It is helpful to label the bags to match the areas before taking the sample. Soils may be sent in dry or wet.

4 Send the samples to a soil testing service that includes a cation exchange capacity test (CEC). Extension services usually do not provide this service. Tests based only on the pH give no information about what nutrients are available to the plants.

BALANCED SOIL

Oxygen	4 - 5%
Humus	2.5 - 5.0%
Calcium	65 - 75%
Magnesium	12 - 20%
Potassium	3 - 7.5%
Phosphate	250 - 375 PPM
Sulfate	25 - 50 PPM
Nitrogen	20 - 40 PPM
Sodium	0.5 - 3.0%
Salt	400 PPM or less
Chlorides	80 - 120 PPM
Boron	0.8 - 2.0 PPM
Iron	200 PPM or more
Manganese	50 - 125 PPM
Copper	2 - 5 PPM
Zinc	10 - 20 PPM

% = percentage of available nutrients

PPM = parts per million

RECREATING THE FOREST FLOOR

The next step in becoming organic is to recreate the forest floor in all your beds, veggie gardens, and ornamental gardens. Pastures and turf also need to have the components of the forest floor.

A natural forest floor cross section looks like this: the top 2-4" is mulch—leaves, twigs, bark, dead plants, dead bodies of animals, and animal manure. Below that is 1-2" of 1-year-old organic matter and well-broken-down humus. Below that is a mixture of humus and the rock particles of the area. Minerals are contained in the humus and in the broken-up pieces of the base rock material. Below that is the subsoil. Earthworms, insects, and roots are mixed all throughout the layers. The top 7" of the forest floor is the area that is the most well-aerated and host to the bulk of soil biology. That layered structure, transitioning down from rough mulch to subsoil, is exactly what we want to create in the vegetable garden and in the ornamental garden.

This very definite layering of rough mulch on top of humus and native soil is nature's way of covering, protecting, and stimulating the soil. Why then should we not do the same thing in our cultivated gardens? Nowhere in the wild will Mother Nature allow the ground to be bare. Well—except for deserts and naturally eroded areas.

There are several ways to create a manmade "forest floor." The easiest way is to take the leaves from your own property or from the plastic bags stupid neighbors have left along the street and dump them onto bare areas in the planting beds. The depth of this raw material can range from 8-12 inches. This easy method can also be done with hay, tree chips, and most any raw organic material. Fine-textured matter such as sawdust, if used at all, should be applied in thinner layers since there is less air space between the small pieces and therefore less oxygen and carbon dioxide exchange at the soil surface. It's better to compost fine-textured materials such as sawdust or other fresh materials before using them on the beds.

A better way to create the "forest floor" is to use partially completed compost. The texture of the material will be better and the resulting improvement to the soil will be faster. Partially completed compost means you can still identify a portion of the raw materials. The texture is better because a mix of large and small particles and decomposed particles will exist. Soil improvement will be faster because of the high population of beneficial microorganisms. I use partially completed compost as mulch at a depth of 4-6".

To go a step farther, apply a layer of completed compost on the bare soil at a depth of 1-2" and cover the compost with a thick blanket (3-6") of shredded native-wood chips, hardwood bark, pine needles, cypress mulch, or hay. Pine bark can be used, but it is my least favorite choice because its flat pieces can plate to seal off oxygen and it can move around easily from wind and water. If pine bark must be used, avoid the fine-textured material and use only large scale bark.

I do not recommend mulches made from paper, plastic, or gravel unless you have no source of vegetative materials. Various mulching methods will work to keep the soil temperature and mois-ture correct, prevent wind and water erosion, and stimulate the life in the soil. Covering the bare soil with mulch is probably the single most important aspect of organic gardening.

Here's the ideal way to replicate the "forest floor."

STEP 1: Aerate by punching holes in the ground.

STEP 2: Spray the soil with fish emulsion, seaweed, and some biological stimulator.

STEP 3: Apply a light coating of earthworm castings—just enough to barely cover the soil.

STEP 4: Apply a 1" layer of finished compost.

STEP 5: Apply a 4" layer of hardwood bark mulch or nature tree chips.

Note: As a precaution, it's wise to avoid piling the mulch up onto the trunks of plants. If the mulch is kept constantly wet, it can cause trunks to rot.

We'll never be able to do as good a job as Mother Nature in creating the forest floor, but we can come pretty close.

BIODIVERSITY

I'm a very lucky person. In 1987 I met a fellow who not only became a friend but introduced me to the organic way of life. Malcolm Beck, a longtime organic gardener and farmer from San Antonio, taught me how to make compost. He also taught me that every living thing will sooner or later die and everything that dies rots and recycles its nutrients and energy back into the soil. On the surface that sounds pretty morbid, doesn't it? In reality it is fundamental to understanding life, nature, and organics. If dead things didn't rot, this earth would be several thousand feet deep in dead bodies and a smelly place indeed. Malcolm taught me that the decaying process returns the dead plants and animals back to the earth and into the raw elements from which they were made. These basic mineral elements in their journey back become the nutrition and vitality to feed the next generation of plants, animals, and man. The decaying process is performed by the billions of little creatures in the soil we call microorganisms or microbes. They will do their job with or without our help. In fact, it is almost impossible to stop them. The microorganisms can turn our once-alive organic waste back into fertilizer for our farms, lawns, and gardens. They can, that is, if they are allowed to do so.

Unfortunately, in most cities, vegetative waste such as leaves and grass clippings are usually buried in landfills where these life-sustaining nutrients are locked away from air and the natural life, death, and decay cycle. What could have been a great benefit to the fertility and well-being of the soil has become a great problem.

Dead organic material can be managed into a financial and horticultural benefit. All we have to do is protect, encourage, and stimulate microorganisms and friends like beneficial insects, frogs, toads, lizards, snakes, birds, and

other critical parts of what we lump together into the term "biodiversity." It's simple. Stop killing them!

Nature is not a composite of a bunch of independent pieces. Nature is a whole, a complete whole where everything is related to everything else. Hurting any small part of nature hurts everything and everyone.

All living organisms die and they all rot, and everything that rots provides food and life for the next phase of life. Your compost pile will show this quite clearly if you just watch.

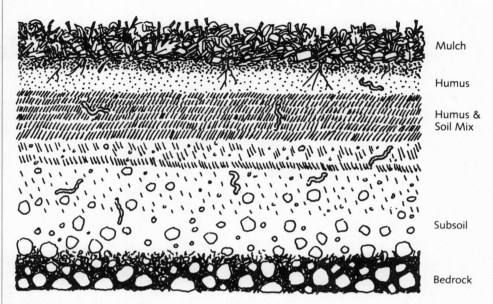

Mulch

Humus

Humus &
Soil Mix

Subsoil

Bedrock

*The forest floor soil crossection consists of
mulch or litter on the surface, decayed organic matter or humus following by minerals
and humus mixed followed by subsoil and
bed rock.*

3

PLANT VARIETIES

PLANT VARIETIES

SELECTING ORNAMENTALS

Books exist in most any region of the country that recommend and explain the best plants to use. Using the native plants of a particular region is becoming more popular and this practice fits together well with an organic program. There are also adapted plants that have been introduced from other parts of the world. I prefer native plants when possible, but the key is to use varieties that will like their new home, making them easy to grow and economical to maintain. In most cases, natives are well adapted and have developed resistance to most harmful insects. Centuries of natural selection have given native plants the ability to survive without pesticides or high levels of fertilization, particularly if they are grown in a healthy soil.

Nature doesn't allow monocultures. Neither should landscape architects or gardeners. When choosing plants (native or introduced), select a variety so that insects and harmful microorganisms will not have one target group. Look at what has happened to millions of American elm trees all over the United States to understand why a diversity of plants is best in the long run. Large monoculture plantings have been devastated.

Another reason to use well-adapted plants in the landscape is water usage and conservation. Water conservation becomes a more serious issue each year. The careful selection of plant materials can make a significant impact on irrigation needs since water requirements vary greatly from plant to plant.

Of course I recommend *Plants of the Metroplex III* and *Howard Garrett's Texas Organic Gardening* for the Texas area, but similar books exist in other parts of the country. Do yourself a big favor by spending some time at your local bookstore, nursery, library, county agent, urban forester's office, or local college or university, learning about the best plants for your area. Then select a variety of plants that will meet your aesthetic and horticultural needs. In conjunction with the organic practices discussed in this book, you should then have the basics for creating a beautiful

landscape, requiring only a minimal amount of maintenance. Note the recommended reading list in the appendix of this book.

My best advice for the selection of trees, shrubs, vines, ground covers, and flowers is to invest in all the local reference books and get the free literature from the botanical gardens, zoos, park departments, and civic garden clubs. Talk to several nurseries, and look at the plants you are considering in different landscape situations. Don't be afraid to try some experiments, but build the framework of the landscape with tough, pest-resistant, adapted varieties.

LANDSCAPING WITH HERBS

Herbs are undergoing a revival. They have been planted for years for their culinary and medicinal uses, but now there's growing interest in another use. Herbs make wonderful landscape plants. They are drought tolerant and grow in almost any well-drained soil. They provide color, texture, and wonderful fragrances. Herbs also give us help with insect control and make excellent companion plants for our vegetable and ornamental plant materials. They fit perfectly into an organic program because they should only be fertilized with natural fertilizers and they should never be sprayed with pesticides.

There are bush-type herbs such as salvia and rosemary. There are excellent ground covers like creeping thyme and pennyroyal mint. There are many beautiful flowering varieties such as yarrow and Texas tarragon. Herbs also have effective insect controlling qualities. Here are some of my favorite herbs to use as landscape plants. I'm not pooh-poohing the medicinal and culinary uses—quite the contrary—I just like for you to have something else to think about.

BASIL (*Ocimum* sp.): There are many types of purple and green basil, and they all make excellent annual plants to use as borders or low masses. Plant from seed or transplants in sun or partial shade. They will usually return from seed each year, but if they don't, buy some more.

BORAGE (*Borago officinalis*): is a beautiful, soft herb that grows to about 3 feet tall. The leaves are gray-green and have whitish bristles. The flowers are star shaped and peacock blue and bloom throughout the summer. Plant in sun or partial shade.

CATNIP (*Nepeta cataria*): is a tall ground cover or shrubby perennial with gray-green, oval leaves. It will reach about 3 feet in height. It has small, white or lavender flowers and is excellent for attracting bees and butterflies—and cats, unfortunately. Sun or partial shade.

CHIVES (*Allium schoenoprasum*): grow in clumps and look a little bit like monkey grass. Onion chives have lavender flowers and round leaves. Garlic chives (*A. tuberosum*) have white flowers and flat leaves. Sun or partial shade.

COMFREY (*Symphytum officinale*): The "healing herb" has large, hairy, 10-15" long leaves. The plant will spread to 3 feet high by 3 feet wide and has lovely, bell-shaped flowers in pink and purple shades that hang gracefully from the stems and last throughout most of the summer. Can grow in sun or shade and should be used as an accent plant or in a large massing. Comfrey will stay evergreen during mild winters but always comes back and establishes into a hardy perennial.

DITTANY OF CRETE (*Origanum dictamnus*): is an excellent herb for hanging baskets or patio containers. It has small, soft, round, gray leaves and tiny purple flowers summer through fall. Best in full sun.

GARLIC (*Allium sativum*): Of course, we have to have garlic to ward off the "evil eye" and the bulbs to make the garlic tea, but it is also a good-looking landscape plant. The foliage of garlic is dark green and the flowers are very interesting as they curve around and fi-nally burst open in the early summer. Best in full sun but can take some shade.

SCENTED GERANIUMS (*Pelargonium* sp.): are excellent landscape plants because of the lovely texture and the nice delicate flowers but more importantly the fragrance when rubbed against or crushed. They come in all sizes and all leaf shapes including deeply cut leaves and those that are soft and velvety.

ELDERBERRY (*Sambucus canadensis*): is a large-growing, beautiful perennial that is often grown for its edible purple-black berries in August through September. It can grow to a height of 10 to 12 feet in most soils and has lovely white flower clusters in the summer. It is also noted for its ability to produce very fine humus soil in the root zone and is a wonderful plant for attracting birds.

LAMB'S EAR (*Stachys byzantina*): is a tough, fuzzy-leafed, gray herb that makes an excellent ground cover to contrast with darker green plants. It can take full sun up to some fairly heavy shade. Lamb's ear's velvet-like foliage and lavender blossoms are delightful to see and to touch.

LEMON BALM (*Melissa officinalis*) is an easy-to-grow, fragrant herb with leaves that are light green and oval with scalloped edges. It has a lemony fragrance and is excellent to interplant among vegetable and landscape plants to look good, help repel pests, and attract bees. Sun or part shade.

LEMONGRASS (*Cybopogon citratus*): is an herb that looks like pampas grass. It grows to a height of about 3 feet, has a wonderful lemon scent, and is excellent for making tea. Although it rarely flowers, it has a lovely texture for a specimen landscape plant. If it freezes, just plant a new one each year. Best in full sun but can take some shade.

LEMON VERBENA (*Aloysia triphylla*): is a wonderfully fragrant addition to the landscape garden as well as the herb garden. It is sensitive to cold so it's best treated as an annual, although it can be used in a pot and brought indoors during the cold months. Best in full sun.

MEXICAN MINT MARIGOLD (*Tagetes lucida*): (See Texas tarragon.)

MINT (*Mentha* sp.): Mints of all kinds make good landscape ground covers but be careful—they all spread aggressively. *Mentha pulegium* is pennyroyal and is an excellent landscape ground cover and reported to repel fleas. Sun or partial shade.

MULLEIN (*Verbascum thapsus*): Common mullein is a wildflower in Texas and looks like a large version of lamb's ear but is more upright and has larger foliage. It also has yellow, white, or purple flowers depending on the variety. Also called flannel leaf or old man's flannel, mullein is a distinctive specimen plant to use in the garden. Full sun to partial shade.

PERILLA (*Perilla frutescens*): is an easy-to-grow annual with dark burgundy leaves. Growth habits are similar to that of coleus or basil. In fact, it looks a great deal like opal basil. However, it is pe-

rennial and can spread aggressively. It can be planted from seed or from transplants and will reseed easily each year. It looks beautiful in contrast with gray plants such as dusty miller, wormwood, or southernwood. Sun or part shade.

PINEAPPLE SAGE (*Salvia elegans*): has beautiful, red flowers in the late summer or fall. It perennializes through all but the hardest winters in the south and grows in sun or shade. It's best to use as a tall-growing annual in cooler climates.

ROSEMARY (*Rosmarinus officinalis*): is a beautiful, gray-green shrub that can grow to a height of 4 feet. It will freeze in hard winters but it is worth replanting every year if necessary. Rosemary has a marvelous pinelike fragrance and beautiful light blue flowers. The low-growing groundcover type is *rosemary prostratus*.

SAFFRON (*Crocus sativus*): The true saffron is an autumn-blooming crocus that resembles ordinary crocus. It has lavender flowers that show in the fall. The saffron food flavor is made from the red-orange stigmas of the plant. Odena Brannam, "The Herb Lady," tells me it's easy to grow.

SAGE (*Salvia officinalis*): is a very tough, evergreen perennial with grayish-green leaves. The only negative is that it will develop woody growth after a while and need to be replaced. There are several different selections including some that have variegated foliage. Plant in sun or part shade and don't overwater.

SALAD BURNET (*Poterium sanguisorba*): is a compact evergreen herb that will reach 2 feet tall with a rosette shape. The plant provides a pleasant cucumber fragrance and has flowers that form on long stems growing out of the center of the plant. Its lacy, symmetrical shape and nice texture make it a good accent plant. Sun or part shade.

SOUTHERNWOOD (*Artemisia abrotanum*): has delicate-looking, dusty-gray foliage that emits a lemon scent even when uncrushed but stronger when crushed. Full sun is best.

TANSY (*Tanacetum vulgare*): is an easy-to-grow, ferny-leafed herb that blooms with yellow, button-like flowers in the late summer to early fall. Crushed or chopped tansy leaves emit a very bitter taste and are an excellent repellant for ants. Sun or shade.

TEXAS TARRAGON (*Tagetes lucida*): is a substitute for French tarragon and much easier to grow. It has a strong fragrance in the garden and produces a terrific display of yellow-orange blossoms in the late summer and early fall.

THYME (*Thymus vulgaris*): makes an excellent landscape plant, especially the creeping thyme, which makes a beautiful and extremely fragrant groundcover that is particularly effective between stepping stones and on borders. Creeping thyme also works well on retaining walls to flow down over the wall. Full sun is best.

WORMWOOD (*Artemisia* sp.): is another gray-leafed plant that is extremely drought tolerant and is a nice contrast with darker plants. Best in full sun.

YARROW (*Achillea millifolium*): is a very lacy, fern-like evergreen perennial with colorful flowers on tall stalks that bloom in the early summer in white, pinks, and reds.

Most herbs will do best in well-drained beds made from a mix of compost and native soil. The best location is full sun in morning and at least some protection from the hot afternoon sun.

It's amazing how old-fashioned things like organics and herbs are coming back so strongly. And they are coming back simply because they work so well.

Herbs also have effective insecticidal qualities. Here are some of my favorites that can be planted among the other vegetable and ornamental plants to help ward off the listed pests.

Herb	Pests Warded Off
Basil	Flies and mosquitoes
Borage	Tomato worm
Garlic	Aphids, beetles, weevils, borers, spider mites
Henbit	Most insects
Lamium	Potato bugs
Marigold	Many insects
Nasturtium	Aphids, squash bugs, white fly
Pennyroyal	Ants, aphids, ticks, fleas
Peppermint	Ants
Pyrethrum	Most insects
Rosemary	Cabbage moths, beetles, mosquitoes, slugs
Rue	Beetles
Sage	Moths
Spearmint	Ants, aphids
Thyme	Cabbage worms and many other insects
Lavender	Ants
Tansy	Ants
Onion	Cabbage moths
Chives	Many fruit-tree and tomato pests

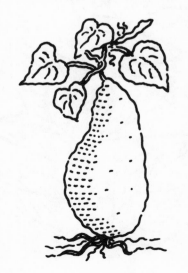

VEGETABLES, FRUITS, NUTS

I t's best to check with the local extension service, local growers and nurseries, and especially local gardeners. Plant a diverse mix of varieties but try to stick with the toughest and best adapted. An excellent source of information will usually be local organic growers and home gardeners. No matter what vegetables you plant, be sure to prepare well-drained and highly organic beds, plant in the proper season, and put a thick mulch layer over all bare soil.

No matter what food crops you decide to try, remember that in most cases these plants are probably not native to your area. For that reason, it's imperative to loosen the soil to provide plenty of oxygen and add lots of compost for additional humus.

Use 100% organic fertilizers liberally if the soil is not biologically healthy and chemically balanced. Supplement the soil treatments by spraying regularly with fish emulsion, seaweed, and biostimulants. Apply rock powders such as colloidal phosphate, greensand, and glacial rock dust annually.

Keep all bare soil mulched at all times, except when new seeds are coming up. Alfalfa hay is the best mulch for vegetable gardens and should be applied 8" thick to allow for settling.

If possible, water by drip irrigation and avoid wetting the foliage too often. Water infrequently but deeply when needed.

Control pests by releasing beneficial insects and by hand removal. Problem infestations can be controlled with various organic products. Check the pest control section starting on page 91 for further details.

WILDFLOWERS

Wildflowers have always been popular in the wild, at least for those people taking the time to stop for a moment and look at them. On the other hand, many people have become frustrated over trying to establish wildflowers on their own properties. Growing wildflowers can be fairly easy but it isn't as simple as throwing seed on the ground and waiting for the spring show. Once again we need to watch what works in nature and try to use those techniques and even improve on them where possible.

Here are some tips to help give you a better chance of a beautiful display of wildflower color next spring.

1 **TIMING:** The time to plant is midsummer through fall. Sowing the seed in late summer best duplicates when nature scatters seed on the earth.

2 **SOIL PREPARATION:** Begin by raking bare soil to a depth of no more than 1". Deep tilling is not only a waste of money but can actually damage the soil and encourage weeds. If grass or weeds exist in the planting site you've chosen, set the mower on its lowest setting and scalp the area down to bare soil.

3 **PLANTING:** First of all, mist or soak the seed in a 1% solution of any biostimulant. Next, distribute the seed uniformly over the area at the recommended rate and rake lightly into the soil to assure good soil/seed contact. It's not essential but is ideal to broadcast a thin ($1/4"$) layer of compost over the seeded area. Water the seeded area thoroughly, but be careful to avoid overwatering, which will erode the loose soil and displace the seed. Many of the wildflower varieties will germinate in the fall and the small plants will be visible all winter. Others will only start to be visible the next spring.

4 **MAINTENANCE:** The most critical step in wildflower planting is to help Mother Nature with the watering if needed. Be sure to provide irrigation (it can be temporary irrigation) the first fall if it is a dry season and again in March and April if it's an unusually dry spring. This is a critical step. The tiny plants need moisture as they germinate and start to grow. They will survive in low water settings once established but they need moisture to get started. The only fertilization I recommend is a light application of earthworm castings, compost, humate, or other 100% organic fertilizers after the seeds germinate and begin to grow in the early spring.

5 **SELECTION:** Some wildflowers are easier to grow than others. Here are the ones I would recommend for the beginner. This list will provide a long display and a wide variety of colors.

Wildflower	Scientific Name	Colors
Black-eyed susan	(*Rudbeckia hirta*)	yellow
Bluebonnet	(*Lupinus texensis*)	blue
Butterfly weed	(*Asclepias tuberosa*)	orange
Coreopsis	(*C. lanceolata*)	yellow
Coreopsis	(*C. tinctoria*)	red & yellow
Cosmos	(*C. bipinatus* & *C. sulphureus*)	multicolors
Engelmann daisy	(*Engelmannia pinnatifida*)	yellow
Evening primrose	(*Oenothera* sp.)	multicolors
Gayfeather	(*Liatris pycnostachya*)	purple
Horsemint	(*Monarda citriodora*)	lavender
Indian blanket	(*Gaillardia pulchella*)	red & yellow
Indian paintbrush	(*Castilleja indivisa*)	orange
Indian paintbrush	(*Castilleja purpurea*)	purple
Lemon mint	(*Monarda citriodora*)	purple
Maximilian sunflower	(*Helianthus maximiliani*)	yellow
Mexican hat	(*Ratibida columnaris*)	red & yellow
Ox-eyed daisy	(*Chrysanthemum leucanthemum*)	white
Purple coneflower	(*Echinacea purpurea*)	purple
Snow on the mountain	(*Euphorbia bicolor*)	white
Tahoka daisy	(*Machaeranthera tanacetifolia*)	purple
White yarrow	(*Achillea millifolium*)	white
Gold yarrow	(*Achillea filipendulina*)	yellow

4

PLANTING TECHNIQUES

PLANTING TECHNIQUES

DRAINAGE

Proper drainage isn't an option—it's a must. If a site doesn't drain, it won't work. Biological activity and chemical exchange will be slowed or stopped—it's that simple. Drainage can be accomplished with surface and/or underground solutions. The best situation includes both. Any system that works is a good system. There are many organic products that will improve the physical structure and the drainage of any soil, but it's still a great benefit to start any project with grading and drainage devices that will get rid of excess water as quickly as possible.

In residential and commercial projects, I recommend and use underground drain lines (perforated PVC pipe) set in gravel for hard-to-drain areas. Using pipe and gravel to drain tree holes can often be the difference between the success and the failure of newly planted plants. A ditch filled with gravel to the soil's surface is an excellent and inexpensive tool to drain water from a low spot. This provides an effective method of drainage.

TREE PLANTING

Trees are the most important landscape element and the only element that actually increases significantly in value after planting. They are the structural features of the landscape and, besides being pleasing to look at and walk under, provide significant services such as blocking undesirable views, shading the ground and other plants, providing protection for wildlife, improving the soil, and providing delightful seasonal beauty.

It is for all these reasons that trees need to be planted correctly so that their root systems develop properly, providing a long, healthy life with a minimum of problems.

Here's how to plant trees organically.

DIG AN UGLY HOLE: A wide, rough-sided hole should be dug exactly the same depth as the height of the ball but much wider than the ball, especially at the surface of the ground. The width of the bottom of the hole is not important. The sides of the hole should be rough and jagged, never slick or glazed.

RUN A PERK TEST: Fill the hole with water and wait until the next day. If the water level doesn't drop substantially overnight, the tree should be moved to another location, or the drainage should be fixed. Tree planting holes must drain well for proper root development and overall health. Adding a tablespoon of liquid seaweed to the perk test water is a good idea. This will help the microbial activity to get started in the wall area of the tree hole.

BACKFILL WITH EXISTING SOIL: Backfill only with the soil that came from the hole. When the hole is dug in solid rock, topsoil from the same area should be used. Some native rock mixed into the soil is beneficial. Topsoil from the immediate area should be used for the top 6-12" of backfill if possible. Do not add sand, bark, peat moss, compost, or other materials to the backfill. Remove burlap from the top of the ball as well as all nylon, plastic string, and even wire mesh. Burlap can be left on the sides of the ball. Container trees will usually be pot-bound. Slash and tear the outer roots away from the ball. This loosening of the roots is a critical step in the planting procedure of container trees but should not be done to ball and burlapped trees. After settling the native soil in the hole with water (not by tamping), cover the surface of the hole with 1/2"-1" of finished compost. Cover the compost with 3-4" of shredded native-tree chips or hardwood bark.

DO NOT WRAP OR STAKE: Wrapping tree trunks is a waste of money, looks unattractive, harbors insects, and leaves the bark weak when removed. Staking and guying is usually unnecessary. If the tree has been planted properly, staking is a waste of money and detrimental to the proper trunk development of the plant. Staking should only be done as a last resort and never left in place more than one growing season. In areas of the country where sunburn on trunks is a problem, white wash made from water-based, nontoxic paint is much better than wrapping. As the white wash wears off, the bark will slowly adjust to the sunlight.

DO NOT OVERPRUNE: It's an old wife's tale that limb pruning must be done to compensate for the loss of roots during transplanting or planting. Most trees fare much better if all the limbs and foliage are left intact. The more foliage, the more food can be produced to help build the root system. The health of the root system is the key to the overall health of trees. The only trees that seem to respond positively to thinning at the time of transplanting are densely foliated evergreen trees collected from the wild. Plants purchased in containers definitely need no pruning when planted, and no deciduous trees need pruning at planting.

MULCH THE TOP OF THE BALL: Do not plant grass all the way in to the trunk of the tree. Leave the area above the top of the ball unplanted and mulch with 1" of compost and 3" shredded hardwood bark, wood chips, or hay. The compost will act as a slow-release fertilizer as well as a mulch. The reason to avoid grass above the tree ball is to elimi-

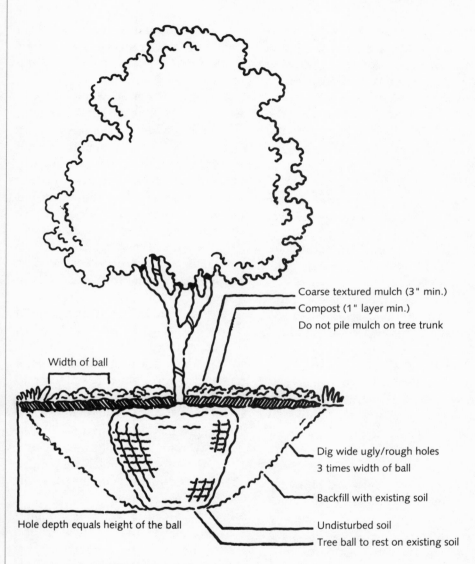

Coarse textured mulch (3" min.)
Compost (1" layer min.)
Do not pile mulch on tree trunk

Width of ball

Dig wide ugly/rough holes
3 times width of ball

Backfill with existing soil

Hole depth equals height of the ball

Undisturbed soil
Tree ball to rest on existing soil

Organic Tree Planting Detail

nate the competition for water, nutrients, and especially oxygen. As the tree establishes, it's okay for the grass to grow in toward the trunk, although maintaining a mulched area around the trunk of the tree is healthy and helps keep the weed eaters and mowers away from the trunk.

LAWN PLANTING

Lawn planting techniques can be quite simple and economical, or complicated and wasteful. If you follow these simple techniques, your lawn establishment can be successful and affordable.

Soil preparation should include the hand or mechanical removal of all weeds, debris, and rocks over 2" in diameter from the surface of the soil. Rocks within the soil are no problem because they actually aid drainage. Herbicides are unnecessary and not recommended.

Lightly till or scarify the topsoil to a depth of 2", rake smooth, and gently slope to prevent ponding of water. Deep rototilling is unnecessary and a waste of money unless the soil is heavily compacted. In fact, rototilling can actually damage the soil.

Although the introduction of some organic material can be beneficial, soil amendments in general are unnecessary and only on solid rock areas is the addition of native topsoil needed. Imported foreign topsoil is a waste of money and can cause a perched (trapped) water table and lawn problem. Poor drainage is often a result of this procedure.

Prior to seeding, spray the soil with a biostimulant and treat the seed with one of the same products. Apply a light application of organic fertilizer at the time of the first mowing.

Severely sloped areas should have an erosion protection material, such as jute mesh, placed on the soil prior to planting. Follow the manufacturer's recommendations for installation.

Some people recommend and use herbicides and soil sterilants to kill weeds prior to planting. I don't! These chemicals are extremely hazardous and hard on the soil. Use a little more elbow grease and dig the weeds out. The weeds' root system will actually help you establish the permanent grasses.

Seeding and hydromulching should be done so that the seed is placed in direct contact with the soil. If hydromulching is used, the seed should be broadcast onto the bare soil first and then the hydromulch blown on top of the seed. One of the worst mistakes I see in grass planting is mixing the seed in the hydromulch. This causes the seed to germinate in the mulch, suspended above the soil, and many of the seeds are lost from drying out.

After spreading seed, thoroughly soak the ground and lightly water the seeded area as necessary to keep it moist. As the seed germinates, watch for bare spots. Reseed these bare areas immediately. Continue the light watering until the grass has solidly covered the area. At this time begin the regular watering and maintenance program. Deep, infrequent waterings are best. Light watering done every day or every other day causes all kinds of problems, such as shallow roots, salt buildup in the top soil, and high water bills.

Solid sod blocks should be laid joint to joint after applying a liquid stimulant to the ground. Grading, leveling, and smoothing prior to planting is very important. Sod can be rolled with a heavy hand-roller after planting, although compaction from this technique bothers me. The joints between the blocks of sod can be filled with compost or granite sand to give a more finished look to the lawn, but this step is optional.

ORGANIC BED PREPARATION

NEW BEDS WITH NO GRASS OR OLD BEDS: No excavation—add 6" compost, organic fertilizer (2 lbs./100 sq. ft.), rototill to a total overall depth of 8". Top-dress bed with 3" layer of shredded hardwood bark or native-tree-chip mulch after planting.

NEW BEDS IN GRASSY AREA: Remove existing sod with sod cutter to a depth of 2¹/₂", add 6" compost, organic fertilizer (2 lbs./100 sq. ft.), rototill to a total depth of 8". Top-dress beds with 3" layer of shredded hardwood bark or native-tree-chip mulch after planting.

AZALEA BED PREP: Mix 50% shredded hardwood bark and 50% finished compost, 1 lb. of sulfur, and 2 lbs. of copperas (iron sulfate) per cubic yard. Thoroughly moisten the mixture prior to placing in the bed. Excavate 3" and place 15" of the above mix into the beds. The top should be flat and the sides sloped at a 45 degree angle. No top-dressing mulch is needed, but ¹/₂"

of the mix should cover the top of the ball.

SHRUB, GROUND COVER, VINE, AND FLOWER PLANTING

Preparing landscape and garden beds correctly the first time allows the plants to establish more quickly, grow faster, and stay healthier. Many people get frustrated with the lack of results and either give up gardening or spend huge sums of money ripping out the plants, preparing the beds correctly, and replanting. So save some time, money, and aggravation by following these steps:

REMOVE WEEDS AND GRASS: Excavate beds to a depth necessary to remove all weeds and grass, including rhizomes. 2¹/₂" deep is usually enough. Do not use herbicides to kill grass and weeds.

ADD TOPSOIL FOR PROPER GRADE: If needed, add native topsoil to all beds to within 2" of the adjacent finished grade. Avoid foreign, unnatural materials, including soils that are different from the existing.

ADD COMPOST: Cover areas to be planted with a 6" depth of properly decomposed and composted organic material. In other words, use compost. Avoid the use of peat moss, raw barks, and other raw materials.

ADD MINERALS: Most soils have plenty of minerals, but in some soil the addition of granite sand, greensand, rock phosphate, lava sand, or gypsum can be beneficial. Soil tests should be made prior to adding these materials.

ADD FERTILIZER: An application of an organic fertilizer should be broadcast at 20 lbs./1000 sq.ft. onto the planting bed prior to tilling. An application of a biostimulant is also beneficial.

TILL COMPOST TOGETHER WITH NATIVE SOIL: Till the compost and the existing topsoil together until the compost/soil mixture is 8-10" deep. Ground cover beds do not have to be tilled as deeply.

NEVER TILL WET SOIL: Working wet soil will squeeze the soil particles together, eliminating the air spaces needed for good tilth and soil life.

RAISE THE BEDS: The top of the beds should be flat and higher than surrounding grades with sloped edges for drainage. This lifting happens naturally if proper amounts of compost are added to the beds.

MOISTEN BEDS BEFORE PLANTING: Planting beds should be moistened before the planting begins. Do not plant in dry soil because the young roots can become dehydrated quickly.

TEAR POT-BOUND ROOTS: Pot-bound plants can resist water and cause the growth of deformed and unhealthy root systems. Cut or tear the mat of circling roots at the outside edge of the root ball.

PLANT THE PLANT LEVEL: Set the plants so that the top of the rootball is even with the surrounding soil. Setting the plant too low may cause drowning and deprivation of oxygen. Planting too high can cause the upper roots to dry out. Quick root development will be aided by spraying the roots of plants with a biostimulant solution before planting.

MULCH BEDS AFTER PLANTING: A minimum 3" layer of organic mulch should be placed on the soil after planting; shredded hardwood bark or native tree chips for shrubs and ground cover and compost for annuals and perennials.

Note: If it sounds simple, it is!

PREPARATION OF FARM LAND

Agricultural land is handled much the same as the home vegetable garden or landscape. It's just that the size is greater, and it's more critical to be as efficient as possible with input costs. Let nature do as much of the work as possible.

Mechanical aeration and products with low cost per acre such as green manure cover crops, humates, and biological stimulators are important tools.

Compost can be an important tool for farm land. Less-than-finished compost is best for agricultural fields. Compost that has only been turned one time is best so the completion of the composting process happens in the soil. Application should be done, if possible, 6 weeks prior to planting. Compost should be lightly tilled into the soil so that the escaping nitrogen is captured in the soil.

Aeration is critical. For tightly compacted soil, use a chisel plow or aerator to break through the hard pan. Mechanical aerifying machines such as Air-

Way are quite effective. Liquid products that can speed up the tilth improvement process include Pene-Turf, Agrispon, Medina, Bioform, AgriGro, and Nitron A-35.

GARDENING BY THE MOON

Plants that produce on the top of the ground—plant in the light of the moon.

People who garden by the moon believe that the same gravitational force that moves the tides up and down also has significant influence on plant growth. Most moon gardeners believe that the increasing light of the moon benefits those plants that bear fruit above the ground. Conversely, they believe that when the moon is on the wane, and its light and gravitational pull are on the decrease, the earth's gravity kicks in again, and the plants that produce below the ground are benefited.

The *Old Farmer's Almanac* says that flowering bulbs and vegetables that bear crops below ground should be planted during the dark of the moon. That is, from the day after it is full to the day before it is new again. Anything like radishes, onions, potatoes, etc. that grow underneath the ground will grow larger and produce better. If you plant on the new moon, they'll grow tall and bloom, but the veggies won't be good.

Planting should not be done when the moon is absolutely dark because that's when plants should rest. The new moon seems to be a good time to kill weeds because they won't grow back.

Moon gardeners have different opinions, and you can hardly find two who

plant the same way. And they all think they're right, because whichever way they choose seems to work.

If you have the time to pay attention to cosmic forces as shown to us by the moon and stars, gardening by the moon can be fun and very productive.

MULCHES

Mulch is a critical ingredient in any organic program. It helps conserve moisture, buffers the soil from temperature extremes, shades out weeds, looks nice, and increases the tilth of the soil. It also supplies food for soil life and nutrients for the soil, keeps raindrops from compacting the soil, keeps the sun from burning the humus out of the soil, and prevents erosion.

After planting any kind of plant—tree, shrub, ground cover, flower, or vegetable, all bare soil should be covered with at least 3" of mulch. Mulch is not a soil amendment mixed into the soil—it's a covering placed on top of the finished planting bed after the plants have been installed.

Not all mulches are created equal. There are many acceptable mulches but they vary in quality and effectiveness. One of the best top-dressing mulches is partially decomposed compost. I discovered the benefit of this material at home as a result of being too impatient to wait on my own compost pile to finish its decomposition. The not-quite-finished compost has larger particles and does a good job of mulching and letting oxygen breathe through to the soil surface.

Grass clippings make a pretty good mulch, but only if mixed with leaves and other debris. I don't recommend lawn grass clippings as a mulch by themselves because the flat blades plate and seal off the soil's gas exchange. Straw and hay are excellent forms of mulch even though they are coarse in appearance. Alfalfa is the best hay mulch because of its nutrient value and the presence of *triacontanol*, a growth regulator. Another excellent mulch is shredded hardwood bark. This good-looking material comes from the lumber industry in places like East Texas and is simply tree bark that has been run through a hammer mill. This smashing action gives the bark its fibrous texture. It's that texture that helps to hold it in place in your beds even on slopes but still allows air to circulate down to the soil. A less expensive and even better material is shredded native-wood chips. Chips straight from the tree trimmer's truck are large and too coarse for most uses, but once shredded into a finer texture they look good and work beautifully. An added benefit of the tree-chip mulch is that the buds and cambium layer contain protein, which contains nitrogen.

Not all bark makes a good top-dressing mulch. For example, the fine to medium grades of pine bark make, at best, a second-rate mulch. Pine bark consists of flat pieces that plate together and seal off the oxygen from the soil. Pine bark often washes or blows away. The tars and resins in pine bark can also inhibit proper aerobic degradation. The

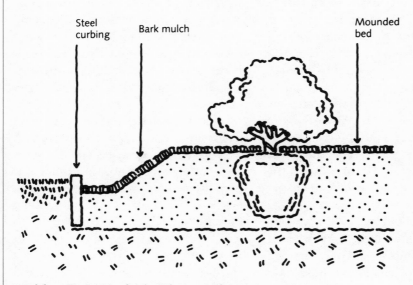

Steel curbing   Bark mulch   Mounded bed

Mulches: To Be Used After Planting. Planting beds should be raised, sloped down on the edge and covered with a thick blanket of mulch.

only pine bark that makes a decent mulch is the large, nugget size because it will at least hold in place well. The large nuggets don't fit together tightly, so air can still circulate around the pieces down to the soil, and large pieces don't rob nitrogen from the soil as fine-particled mulch sometimes does.

Pine needles are a good choice when used as a top-dressing mulch, especially when used in parts of the state where pine trees are native. There's also an economic advantage when the material is locally available and can be gathered from the forest floor, although care should be taken not to deplete the organic matter in any natural setting.

Walnut should not be used as a mulch until fully composted. The raw material has strong growth-retarding properties.

Sawdust is sometimes used as a mulch, but I don't recommend it unless it has been mixed with coarser materials and composted for a while. Sawdust does make an excellent ingredient for the compost pile.

Pecan shells make a good top-dressing mulch but are much better if composted first with other vegetative materials.

Shredded cypress chips make good mulch but tend to mat and seal off oxygen a little more than I would like. They break down very slowly and are more expensive than most other mulches.

I do not recommend the artificial mulches such as plastics and fabrics, nor do I recommend gravel as a mulch. The nonorganic mulches don't biodegrade and don't return anything to the soil.

Real mulches of organic matter, when applied in appropriately thick layers, will eliminate weeding and cultivation, eliminate soil compaction, save money on irrigation, preserve and stimulate the soil microorganisms and earthworms, and maintain the ideal soil temperature. In the heat of summer, the soil surface under a proper layer of mulch will be around 82-85°. The temperature of bare soil can be in excess of 120°.

Some alleged experts say that whenever a highly carbonaceous mulch such as bark mulch is used, decomposition organisms will steal nitrogen from the soil unless a fertilizer that supplies 1 lb. of nitrogen for each 100 lbs. of mulch is added. Not true! For years I have mulched with hay, bark, tree chips, etc. without supplying extra nitrogen and have never observed any symptoms of nitrogen deficiency as long as the mulch stays on the top of the soil. When raw organic matter is tilled into the soil, there usually is nitrogen draft. Finished compost only should be tilled into the soil. People who still till peat moss and bark into the soil are behind the times.

Conclusion: use compost to prepare planting beds, and use a coarse-textured mulch on the surface of the soil after the plants have been installed.

COMPOST: Compost is an excellent mulch for annuals and perennials and for use as a top-dressing mulch for newly planted trees. A light layer of compost is also beneficial on new shrub and groundcover beds prior to the addition of the coarse mulch. Compost is magic! At least it contains nature's magic. It is also effective to use around sick trees and other plants to help them recover. Compost is nature's fertilizer.

SHREDDED HARDWOOD BARK: Hardwood bark is an excellent mulch material for ornamental planting beds. It is fibrous and has coarse and fine particles, so it grows fungi quickly. The microbes lock the material together to prevent washing and blowing but still allow air transfer to the soil. Hardwood mulch is one of the best choices to use above newly planted trees, shrubs, and other permanent plants.

CYPRESS CHIPS: Shredded cypress mulch is a good, long-lasting product but more expensive than most other mulch products.

HAY: Hay is the best mulch for vegetable gardens. Alfalfa is the best choice—bermuda is the worst. Layers 8-10" thick give the best results and work best to prevent weed seed germination.

DECO BARK: The large size deco bark is good mulch to use for shrubs and ground covers. Deco bark can be used along with the proper bed preparation to achieve full ground-cover establishment in one growing season. The large size of the deco bark allows air to flow around the large pieces and down to the soil and to the plants' roots.

NATIVE TREE CHIPS: Tree chips are good to use in large areas as a natural ground cover. If ground into smaller pieces, they can be used to mulch all types of plants. Shredded tree-chip mulch, because of the buds and cambium layer under the bark, contains more nitrogen than most mulches and therefore doesn't take any nitrogen from the soil.

PINE BARK: Pine bark is used widely as a bed preparation material but shouldn't be. Bark is good to use as a topdressing mulch in groundcover and shrubs if the pieces are large (at least 2-3"). Small size bark chips tend to plate together and seal off the soil from oxygen. They also have a tendency to wash and blow away. Very fine particles of mulch can sometimes rob some of the nitrogen from the soil.

PINE NEEDLES: Pine needles are an excellent mulch to use in most planting beds, but they are certainly more appropriate when used in areas where pine trees grow, so they don't look out of place.

"Mulching by itself cannot make up for the shortfall of fertility in the soil."

Dr. William A. Albrecht

"But it can certainly take you in the right direction."

J. Howard Garrett

ORGANIC MULCHES

Organic Mulches	Rating	Application	Remarks
Pine bark (large size)	Good	3" deep in ornamental beds.	Works well but some people don't like the look.
Pine Bark (small to medium)	Poor	Use as a last resort only.	Washes and blows around. Flat pieces tend to seal off oxygen from the soil.
Cedar chips	good	Best to use after composting a while.	Decoiled cedar flakes are the very best greenhouse flooring material.
Coffee grounds	Poor	Best to use in compost pile.	Slightly acid. Will blow and wash away.
Compost	Excellent	Use partially decomposed material 3-5" thick.	Save the more decomposed to till directly in the soil.
Corncobs (ground)	Good	Apply 3" thick.	Availability may be a problem.
Cornstalks (chopped)	Fair	Apply 4-6" deep in vegetable gardens.	Very coarse texture.
Cottonseed hulls	Good	Apply 3-4" deep	Have fertilizer value similar to cottonseed meal. Very light and tend to blow around.
Cypress chips	Good	Apply 3" deep.	Can seal off oxygen. Expensive.
Lawn clippings	Poor	Better to mix into compost pile.	Good source of nitrogen. Flat pieces plate and seal off oxygen.
Leaves	Good	Best run through a chipper before applying 3" deep.	Blowing and washing can be a problem.
Manure	Fair	Apply only after composting.	Fresh manure can burn plants and can contain salts and weed seeds.

Organic Mulches Continued

Organic Mulches	Rating	Application	Remarks
Pecan shells, Peanut shells, Rice hulls	Good	Apply 3" deep. Better to compost first with other materials.	Inexpensive, becoming more available, high in nitrogen.
Peat moss	Terrible	Don't use; the worst mulch choice.	Expensive, blows and washes away.
Pine needles	Excellent	Apply 3-5" thick on vegetable gardens and ornamental beds.	Looks best when used in association with pine trees.
Sawdust	Poor	Use in the compost pile, not as a mulch.	Small pieces seal off oxygen exchange when used as a mulch.
Seaweed	Fair	Not readily available but works well.	Watch for salt content. Decomposes slowly.
Straw, hay	Excellent	Apply 4-5" deep in ornamental beds, 8-10" deep in vegetable garden.	Use for winter protection. Alfalfa is the best. Bermuda grass is the worst.
Shredded hardwood bark	Excellent	Apply 3-4" deep in ornamental beds.	Best mulch of all for use on sloped areas.
Shredded native native tree chips	Excellent	Apply 3-4" deep in ornamental beds.	Almost as good as hardwood but cheaper.
Gravel	Poor	Best used at 3-6" in utility areas.	Large, decorative stones are good for use in shady landscape areas.
Lava rock	Fair	Apply 3-5" deep.	Avoid using in large areas— too harsh.

5

MAINTENANCE

MAINTENANCE
WORKING WITH NATURE'S SYSTEMS

NATURAL TREE CARE

PRUNING: Is it time to thin my trees and cut off the lower limbs? My answers to these common questions might surprise you. There seems to be an abundance of curious tree-pruning advice around. Let's try to straighten it out.

Pruning too much is the most common mistake. Few trees need major pruning every year. Other than some fruit trees, few trees need annual thinning and, unless lower limbs are a physical problem, they should be left on the tree.

Timing: Landscape trees can be pruned any time of the year, but the best time is from fall to late winter. Fruit trees should be pruned from midwinter up until bud break. Certain fruit trees like peach trees, for example, should only be pruned just before bud break because pruning induces bud break and flowering. Early flowers and late freezes spell no fruit.

Amount of Pruning: Pruning trees is part science and part art. Don't try to change the character and overall, long-term shape of a tree, and don't remove lower limbs to raise the canopy. Low growing limbs exist for a reason. It's very unnatural to strip tree trunks bare. If you think that looks good, think again. Remove all dead, diseased, broken, or damaged limbs and the weakest of crossing limbs. Remove limbs that grow toward the center of the tree and limbs that are dangerous or physically interfere with buildings or activities. Thinning to eliminate a certain percentage of the foliage is usually a mistake. Heavy thinning of a tree's canopy throws the plant out of balance, inviting wind and ice storm damage. The resulting stress attracts diseases and insect pests. Gutting is rarely if ever appropriate.

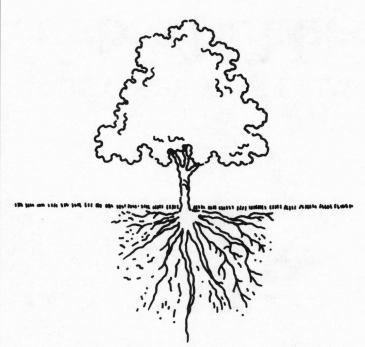

How people think tree roots grow.

How tree roots really grow.

Pruning Cuts: Pruning cuts should be made with sharp tools. Hand tools such as bow saws, Japanese pruning saws, loppers, and pole pruners are good for small limbs. Chain saws can be used for larger limbs, but only with great care and a thorough understanding of the equipment.

Flush cuts should be avoided. Cuts leaving a $1/16$" stub are also bad. Pruning cuts should be made at the point where the branch meets the trunk, just outside the branch collar. The branch collar will have the appearance of a small stub after pruning. The branch collar stub will be $1/8$-$1/4$" on small limbs but can be several inches wide on large limbs.

It's scientific fact that cutting into or removing the branch collar causes problems. Flush cuts create large, oval-shaped wounds and encourage decay. They also destroy the natural protective zone between the trunk and the branch and can cause several serious tree problems including discolored wood, decayed wood, wet wood, resin pockets, cracks, sun injury, cankers, and

slowed growth of new wood. Proper cuts are round, smaller, and heal much faster. Peach, plum, apricot, and other fruit trees are particularly sensitive to flush cuts. Many fruit tree insects and disease problems are related to improper pruning cuts. Long branch stubs are also detrimental and should be avoided.

Wound Dressings: Research by Alex Shigo, Carl Whitcomb, and the U. S. Forest Service has shown that pruning paint and wound dressings have no benefit and can be harmful by slowing the healing process. Healthy tissue needed for callus can be damaged or killed by pruning paint or dressings. Trees have defense cells, much like white blood cells in mammals. Lignin cells are produced on the backside of a wound to naturally prevent diseases from entering fresh cuts. Just as a cut finger heals faster when exposed to the air, so does a tree wound.

Cavities: Cavities in trees are voids where fungi have rotted healthy material. They are usually the result of physical injury to the bark. Removing only the decayed material is the remedy. Fillers such as concrete and foam are only cosmetic and not recommended. When removing decayed matter from cavities, be careful not to cut or punch into the living tissue. Injuries to healthy tissue can introduce decay into the healthy wood. When cavities hold water, drain tubes are sometimes inserted to release water. Bad idea. Drain tubes puncture the protective barrier between the rotted and healthy wood and allow decay to expand. I don't recommend trunk

Proper cut leaving branch collar

Improper flush cut

injector systems for fertilizer and insect control because of their puncture wounds.

Cabling: Weak crotches between limbs can sometimes be stopped from splitting by installing cables horizontal to the ground so the natural movement of the tree is not completely stopped. Cabling used to hold up low growing limbs is poor tree care and a waste of money. Cabling can be very dangerous and should only be done by professional arborists.

As a final note, the tree chips and sawdust resulting from pruning should not be hauled away. The large pieces should be used for firewood and the limbs and foliage should be shredded and used as mulch under trees or mixed into a compost pile.

FERTILIZING: Since all plants require food, trees should not be overlooked when a landscape is fertilized. The easiest way to fertilize trees is in conjunction with the general fertilization of the grass and planting beds beneath the trees. The feeder roots are near the surface, and the tree will utilize whatever nutrients are there. Remember that over 80% of a tree's root system is in the top 12-18" of soil.

Putting fertilizer in holes drilled throughout the root zone is not recommended for general fertilization, but is effective for a specific deficiency such as chlorosis. The roots will take the pure material (sulfur, iron, or magnesium, for example) away from the cores as needed.

A good balanced, organic fertilizer is perfect for establishing a healthy condition for trees. Fertilizer should be applied two or three times a year, as with other plantings. Placing a layer of compost over the entire root zone of the tree (and beyond) will also help greatly to feed the soil and thus the tree. Healthy plants will repel insects and diseases, reducing or eliminating the need for pest control products. Periodic applications of foliar food are also beneficial. Good products include fish emulsion, seaweed, and various biostimulants.

AERATION: Mechanical hole punching is recommended for tree care, especially in clay or other heavy soils. Oxygen is one of the most important elements in healthy soil. Air penetration helps greatly to stimulate microbial activity and root growth.

PEST CONTROL: Occasionally trees need to be sprayed to control certain pests, or to give them a little extra nutrient punch. In an organic program, this can be accomplished in one step, reducing the cost once again. A mixture of fish emulsion and liquid seaweed (kelp) will help control most harmful insects without killing the beneficial ones. At the same time, the compounds found in the two products act as a foliar fertilizer for the tree. These products are safe and will give impressive results. There is an odor with these products, especially fish emulsion, which lasts about 24 hours but it is no worse than chemical insecticides. Fish products that contain molasses have less odor.

The most persistent pest is the aphid, which is the most prevalent in the spring when trees start their active growth cycle. Aphids damage plants by sucking the juices from tender, new growth. There is a very easy way to control aphids—spray with garlic/pepper tea or soap and water. Pure water blasts followed by the release of ladybugs is my favorite aphid control. Fish emulsion also offers good control of soft-bodied insects. Diatomaceous earth can also be mixed with water or with these other products to help control insects in trees, but it will also kill beneficial insects, so be careful!

Protecting and adding to the beneficial insect population will give effective control of aphids and other harmful insects. Good insects include ladybugs, green lacewings, praying mantids, wasps, mud dobbers, and others.

Taking care of trees using common-sense techniques and safe products is easy and cost effective. The results are better than using chemical treatments, which will destroy many beneficial insects while only reducing a percentage of the target insects. Imagine being able to spray trees without worrying about wind drift, lawsuits, over-application of material, and the real possibility that the environment is being harmed each time a pesticide is applied. That's the beauty of tree care using the natural approach—it is safer and it works!

LAWN CARE

Grass is the most intensely maintained of all plants and indeed the biggest expense in any landscape maintenance budget. It is scalped, mowed, fertilized, sprayed before weeds appear, sprayed after weeds appear, walked on, driven on, and usually abused all during the year. As with all plant types, there are some cost effective, organic approaches for the care of grasses.

MOWING: Many turf areas are mowed too low. When grass is mowed short, the root system is correspondingly too short. That increases the demand for water and food, encourages weeds to germinate, and can cause the lawn to decline.

Generally, turf should be mowed to a height of at least $2^1/_2$" or taller and should not be allowed to grow taller than $1/_3$ again its height. Cutting more than $1/_3$ of the grass blades can cause noticeable damage to the grass, which can take several days to overcome. Golf courses and other playing field turf areas don't always have the luxury of letting the grass grow taller but landscape areas certainly do. Except for the low-growing, dwarf hybrids, bermudagrass and zoysia can be mowed the lowest at $2^1/_2$-3", and cool season and St. Augustine grasses can be mowed at 3-$3^1/_2$".

Another important mowing technique is to leave the grass clippings on the ground—don't bag them and haul them away. This practice wastes time and money and is detrimental to the lawn. There's also an environmental issue related to the crowded condition of municipal landfills. Grass clippings in plastic bags have been responsible for 20-40% of the waste in city dumps.

Grass clippings left on the lawn will decompose rapidly in the presence of water and organic fertilizer, creating food for microbes and the much-needed humus for the soil. Since the organic matter makes the soil healthier, the number of weeds will be reduced. Discarding the grass clippings also throws nutrients away. Tests at the University of Connecticut agricultural experiment station showed, through the use of radioactive isotopes, that nitrogen in grass clippings left on the lawn was back in the growing plants in as short a time as one week.

Scalping a lawn is a waste of time and money. It is also harmful to the lawn. When the soil is exposed through scalping, humus is burned out of the soil, microbes suffer, and weed seed germinate.

AERATION: Aerating the soil is the single most important procedure in establishing soil health and going "organic." Soil will naturally become aerated by the addition of humus and the stimulation of earthworms and microbial activity if given enough time. All you have to do is add compost and organic fertilizers and stop using harsh, synthetic products and nature will take over.

However, most of us want the process to go faster, and the answer is "punching holes" in the ground. These holes can be punched with a stiff-tined turning fork or any spiked tool. The most convenient method is to buy or rent an aerator or hire a landscape contractor to use a mechanical aerator to poke holes all over the yard. Hand work usually has to be done in the beds.

Mechanical aerators are available in all shapes and sizes with many features. Some just punch small holes, others remove cores, and some inject water while punching holes. Some can even punch holes 12" deep. All these machines work. The more holes, the better, and the deeper the holes, the better. Just choose a machine that fits your budget, because the cost ranges greatly. The object is getting oxygen into the soil. When that happens, microbe populations start to increase instantly, natural nitrogen cycles function properly, and nature's wonderful systems are all set in motion. It's not necessary to understand all the systems in great detail—it's only important to respect their presence and let them work for you.

FERTILIZING LAWNS: Another tip for good organic lawn care is to avoid chemical fertilizers, which are usually applied 3, 4, or more times a year. They green up a lawn quickly, but their effect soon falls off as the chemicals are leached out of the soil or washed down the street. Besides, they create a major hardship for the poor guy who's pushing the mower because chemical fertilizers create flushes of heavy growth. Chemical fertilizers feed the plants artificially and do nothing for the soil, so their long-term effect is quite damaging.

Organic fertilizers provide the proper nutrients without damaging the soil. Natural fertilizers only need to be applied 2 or 3 times a year and are safe, even if they are washed away by accident. They release nutrients slowly, feeding the plants only what they need and at the proper time. The result is green, healthy grass with slower, more consistent growth, making it easier to avoid having to catch the grass clippings.

Supplemental feeding of a lawn can be done at any time using liquid foliar materials such as fish emulsion, liquid kelp, and biostimulants. Foliar feeding will prevent the chlorotic look that lawns often have in late summer when the hot, dry days take their toll. It can also be used on grass areas any time to give the color a boost. Foliar feeding can reduce stress damage and improve cold tolerance.

PEST CONTROL: The next lawn care necessity is spraying for all the things that don't belong. Most of the harmful insects, fungi, and bacteria can be controlled with a fish emulsion/liquid kelp mixture or with a baking-soda spray. A healthy soil that drains well is the best long-term control.

Weeds can be controlled with organic products. Building a healthy soil, applying adequate fertilizer and water, and mowing on time will prevent most weeds, but there are no nontoxic herbicides on the market today that are foolproof. The only foolproof method of safely eliminating weeds is hand pulling or mechanical devices.

COMPOSTING LAWNS: Composting helps both in fertilization and weed control. A 1/4-1" layer of compost spread over a lawn once a year will provide the grass most of the nutrients it needs. It is an expensive process compared to cheap chemical fertilizers, but it improves the health of the soil and grass and will act as a buffer to extreme climatic changes and even to harsh chemicals. When funds are limited, composting every other year will usually be adequate.

Compost will also help prevent weeds by increasing the health of the soil. Few noxious weeds will grow in a healthy, balanced soil, and what few do appear are easily removed by hand or spot spraying. Learning to accept a lawn with a mix of grasses, wildflowers, and herbs is not only okay but recommended.

Safe lawn care is critical because the lawn is where the most people-use occurs, and the absence of chemicals means a healthier environment for children, pets, and others. Children are a very special concern but the elderly and ill people of all ages are also particularly sensitive.

RENOVATING A WORN OUT LAWN: For compacted, weedy, unhealthy lawn areas: first mechanically aerate and don't be bashful—tear up the ground. Next, spray the area with a fish, seaweed, and biostimulant mix. Next, apply a 100% organic fertilizer at 20 lbs./ 1,000 sq. ft. For additional help, add 1/4" of compost, which is about 1 cubic yard per 1,300 sq. ft.

SHRUB, GROUND COVER, VINE, AND FLOWER CARE

Shrubs, ground covers, flowers, and vines are the easiest plants to maintain. Sometimes they need light pruning, fertilizing, and even spraying, but they are easily accessible (unlike trees), and do not require intense maintenance (unlike grass).

PRUNING: Pruning shrubs, ground covers, and perennial flowers is really quite simple. Only remove enough growth to keep the plants under control. For example, most ground covers will need to be pruned back once in the early spring to remove the dead stubble, and after that only when they encroach on paved surfaces or other planting areas.

Perennials should be pruned in the late fall or winter to remove the previous year's dead growth. Or, prune opposite the bloom period. For example, prune spring-blooming perennials in the fall and fall-blooming perennials in the spring. Additional heavy pruning after strong flushes of flowers have started to play out will promote a new flush of flower production.

Shrubs will need more frequent pruning to keep them under control. Light, selective pruning is the best technique. Never prune shrubs by removing a large amount of growth or by constantly "boxing" them, which continuously removes the new growth. Not only does it make the shrub look artificial, it will ultimately ruin the usefulness of the plant and weaken the plant by reducing the photosynthetic surface. The exception here, of course, is a formal garden, which does require clipped hedges.

FERTILIZING: As with trees and lawns, landscape beds should be fed with organic fertilizers 2 or 3 times a year. Flowers will usually need supplemental fertilizers like bat guano, blood meal, fish meal, or fish emulsion. Rock phosphate, a natural, organic source of phosphorous, is a good way to boost flower production. Colloidal phosphate is an even better source of natural phosphorous because it is more quickly available to plants.

PEST CONTROL: As a general rule, spraying to kill insects is not necessary and should not be done on a calendar or preventative basis but instead at the first sign of infestation. For example, the annual ritual of applying insecticides in August for grubworms is one of the most blatant wastes of money and sources of pollution in landscape maintenance. Grubs are only damaging enough to treat when 8-10 per sq. ft. are found. Work to improve the soil through aeration and organic fertilizers; use beneficial insects regularly and the least toxic pesticides as a last resort.

COMPOSTING: Compost should be used around shrubs, ground covers, and flowers to help increase soil health, moisture retention, climatic buffering, and weed control. Whenever compost is used as a mulch, it should be spread to a minimum 2" depth. Once the ground is covered with plant growth, a light ($1/2$") application of compost annually is all that's needed.

INTERIOR PLANTS: Interior plants should be planted in well-drained, organic soil. The soil should not be sterile but alive with microorganisms and earthworms. Some of the best fertilizers for interior plants include earthworm castings and kelp meal. They are mild and odor free.

Pests on interior plants are best controlled by using liquid seaweed, Neo-Life soap, garlic tea, and biostimulants. Horticultural oils and pyrethrum products can be used for severe problems.

For success, give your interior plants plenty of light, moderate amounts of water and fertilization, and a gentle misting of water regularly. If your water is alkaline, add 1 tablespoon of vinegar to each gallon of water.

Organic maintenance is really just a matter of copying what nature does when left alone—it allows only adaptable plants to survive, strives to keep the ground covered, and utilizes organic matter in a never-ending cycle. Man has disrupted that cycle over the years, but by using common sense and safe products, the delicate balance can be re-established. Patterning any landscape maintenance program after nature's own cycles will go a long way toward repairing the damage that has been done and will grow more beautiful plants than you ever imagined.

BASIC ORGANIC PROGRAM

SOIL TEST: Have soil tested (exchange capacity test only) to learn the current levels of organic matter, nitrogen, calcium, magnesium, sulfur, phosphates, potassium, sodium, chloride, boron, iron, manganese, copper, and zinc.

AERATION: Mechanically aerate soil at least once a year so that drainage is improved and microbes are stimulated. Not needed after soil is healthy.

PLANTING: Prepare new planting beds by scraping away existing grass and weeds, adding 4-6" of compost, and tilling 3" into the native soil. Good additional ingredients include granite sand, greensand, lava dust, and colloidal phosphate at 20 lbs./1,000 sq. ft. Do not use peat moss or concrete sand.

FERTILIZING: Apply 100% organic fertilizer to all planting areas in early spring at 10-20 lbs./1,000 sq. ft. Repeat every 60 to 90 days during the growing season if phosphorous and potassium levels remain low.

Foliar-feed all plants with a liquid mixture of fish emulsion at 2 oz./gal., liquid seaweed at 1 oz./gal., biostimulant per label directions, and $1/2$ oz. of natural vinegar. For chlorosis add chelated iron and Epsom salts at 1 tablespoon per gallon.

Add bat guano, fish meal, kelp meal, or earthworm castings at 10-20 lbs./ 1,000 sq. ft. to annuals and perennials in the spring and, if phosphorous and potassium are low, every 30-60 days during the growing season. Add a handful of earthworm castings to each hole when planting bulbs or small transplants. Mist or soak bulbs or seeds before planting in a 1% solution of biostimulant.

MULCHING: Mulch all bare soil. For shrubs, trees, and ground covers use 1" of compost and 3" of shredded wood chips or shredded hardwood bark. Mulch vegetable gardens with 8" of wheat straw, or better still, alfalfa hay.

MOWING/TRIMMING: Mow weekly or more often if necessary, leaving the clippings on the lawn. Put occasional excess clippings in compost pile. Do not send bagged clippings to the dump. Do not use weed eaters around trees. Do not scalp lawn in the spring.

WATERING: Adjust schedule seasonally to allow for deep, infrequent waterings in order to maintain an even moisture level. About 1" of water per week in the summer is a good starting point.

WEEDING: Hand-pull large weeds, mulch all bare soil, and work on soil health for overall control. Avoid chemical herbicides, especially pre-emergent types. Full strength vinegar is an effective organic herbicide on hot days. Corn gluten meal is an excellent organic pre-emergent.

PRUNING: Remove dead, diseased, and conflicting limbs. Don't overprune. Don't make flush cuts and don't paint cuts.

INSECT CONTROL:
Aphids and other small insects: Build soil health; release ladybugs in spring and green lacewings in summer and fall. Spray insecticidal soap or garlic/pepper tea if needed.

Caterpillars and bagworms: Bacillus thuringiensis (Bt), Bti 'Israelensis' for mosquitoes.

Slugs, snails, fleas, ticks, chinch bugs, roaches, crickets: Diatomaceous earth/pyrethrum.

Whiteflies: A mix of liquid seaweed and garlic/pepper tea.

Fire ants: Growth regulator baits for large areas, pyrethrum/diatomaceous earth powder on individual mounds. Soapy water is very effective.

Grubworms: Beneficial nematodes and milky spore are effective, but maintaining healthy soil biology is the primary control for grubworms.

Squash and stink bugs: Sabadella.

DISEASES:
Black spot, brown patch, powdery mildew: Best control is prevention through soil improvement and avoidance of high nitrogen fertilizers. Baking soda and liquid copper sprays are effective.

Animal Care Tips

Healthy Pet Diet for Dogs:

50% grain (rice, barley, etc.)

25% meat (rabbit, chicken, etc.)

25% veggies (steamed)

1/8 tsp. food grade kelp (daily)

Healthy Pet Diet for Cats:

50% meat

25% grain

25% veggies (steamed)

1/8 tsp. food grade kelp (daily)

PET FOOD ADDITIVE: For extra help in fighting fleas and internal parasites, mix together equal portions of diatomaceous earth and garlic powder (chopped garlic is better). Sprinkle lightly on pet food daily as you would salt and pepper on your own food.

Don't forget to brush, bathe, and exercise your pets regularly!

SEVEN STEPS IN GOING ORGANIC

The basics of organics is soil improvement. Healthy soil produces healthy plants with very powerful natural insect and disease resistance.

1 Stop catching the grass clippings. Allow the clippings to return to the soil.

2 Stop using synthetic fertilizers and synthetic pesticides.

3 Start using compost, rock powders, and natural fertilizers.

4 Use natural or least toxic pesticides, but only when needed for specific pests.

5 Select native and well-adapted plants and plant at the correct time of year.

6 Mulch all bare soil—a must!

7 Water thoroughly and deeply, but less frequently.

MAKING COMPOST

Compost is a living fertilizer that can be made at home or purchased ready to use. A compost pile can be started at any time of the year. Good ingredients include leaves, hay, grass clippings, tree trimmings, nongreasy food scraps, bark, sawdust, rice hulls, weeds, nut hulls, and animal manure. Mix the ingredients together in a container of wood, hay bales, hog wire, or concrete blocks or simply pile the material on the ground.

The best mixture is 80% vegetative matter and 20% animal waste, although any mix will compost. The ingredients should be a mix of coarse and fine-textured material. Avoid having all the pieces of material the same size since the variety of sizes will help air to move through the pile. Oxygen is a critical ingredient.

Turn the pile at least once a month; more often speeds up the process. Keep the pile moist, roughly the moisture of a squeezed-out sponge, to help the living microorganisms thrive and work their magic.

Compost is ready to use when the ingredients are no longer identifiable. The color will be dark brown, the texture soft and crumbly, and the aroma that of a forest floor. Use compost in all bed preparation and as a high-quality mulch around annuals and perennials.

ORGANIC RECIPES

GARLIC/PEPPER TEA INSECTICIDE:
Liquify 2 bulbs of garlic and 2 hot peppers in a blender ⅓ full of water. Strain
the solids and add enough water to the
garlic/pepper juice to make 1 gallon of
concentrate. Use ¼ cup of concentrate
per gallon of spray. For added strength,
add 2 tablespoons of vegetable oil for
each gallon of water in the sprayer.

BAKING-SODA FUNGICIDE: Mix 4
teaspoons (about 1 rounded tablespoon)
of baking soda and 1 teaspoon of liquid
soap or vegetable oil into one gallon of
water. Spray lightly on foliage of plants
afflicted with black spot, powdery mildew, brown patch, and other fungal diseases. Avoid overusing, and try to keep
out of the soil. Do not mix baking soda
with other sprays.

*Note: Never store home-made brews in
glass or any tightly sealed container.*

MONTHLY ORGANIC MAINTENANCE CALENDAR
JANUARY

PLANT*:
- Fruit and pecan trees, grapes, berries, asparagus, onions, potatoes, English peas, garlic, anemones, & ranunculus.
- Shrubs, vines, balled-and-burlapped or containerized trees.
- Spring flowers and vegetable seeds indoors.
- Complete tulip, daffodil plantings in early January. "Force" bulbs in pots indoors.
- Cold-hardy color: dianthus, pansies, flowering kale, and cabbage (if the weather is mild).
- Transplant plants during dormant period.

FERTILIZE:
- Root stimulator to new shrubs and trees monthly until established.
- Asparagus beds in late January.

PRUNE:
- Shade trees by removing dead and damaged limbs.
- Summer-flowering trees, including crepe myrtles, by removing no twigs larger than a pencil in diameter.
- Evergreen shrubs.
- Fruit trees. However, the best time is just before bud break in late winter.

WATER:
- Spot water any dry areas to avoid plant desiccation.

PEST CONTROL:
- Dormant oil if needed to scale-prone plants such as: oaks, hollies, camellias, euonymus, pecan and fruit trees. Remember that organic pesticides kill good bugs as well as pests.
- Houseplants: mealy bugs, spider mites, scale—spray with biostimulant, liquid seaweed, and mild soap mixture.

ODD JOBS:
- Have soil tests run.
- Turn compost pile monthly or more often and keep moist.
- Plan spring landscape improvement projects and begin construction activities.
- Prepare garden soil by adding missing minerals and mulching bare soil.
- Take mower, tiller, trimmers into shop for repairs before spring.
- Feed the birds!

* *Planting recommendations based on North Texas climate. Check with your local nurseries and extension service for specific varieties and timing in your area.*

FEBRUARY

PLANT*:
- Broccoli, Brussels sprouts, cabbage, cauliflower, onions, English peas, asparagus, potatoes, other cold-tolerant vegetables, and strawberries for harvest next spring.
- Petunias, pansies, pinks, snapdragons, alyssum, calendulas, glads, cannas, and daylilies.
- Fruit trees and berries.
- Transplant existing landscape plants.
- Transplant crowded summer-blooming perennials.

FERTILIZE:
- All planting areas with a 100% organic fertilizer at approximately 20 lbs./1,000 sq. ft. If the soil is already healthy, the rate can be reduced to 10 lbs./1,000 sq. ft.
- Cool-season flowers with earthworm castings, fish meal, and bat guano at 10 lbs./1000 sq. ft.

PRUNE:
- Shade and ornamental trees lightly to remove dead, diseased, and crossing limbs.
- Peaches and plums by 40-50% to encourage 45° angle growth. Grapes, by 80-90%.
- Evergreens and summer-flowering plants.
- Bush-form roses (not climbers).
- Winter-damaged foliage from liriope, ophiopogon, honeysuckle, Asian jasmine, and other ground covers.

WATER:
- Winter annuals and dry soil areas as needed.

PEST CONTROL:
- Giant bark aphids: no treatment needed in most cases.
- Dormant oil for serious infestations of scale insects. Be sure to keep mixture shaken while using and follow label instructions carefully. Use sparingly if at all.

ODD JOBS:
- Adjust and repair sprinkler system.
- Have soil tested. Watch for accumulations of phosphorous.
- Have maintenance equipment repaired for spring use. Sharpen hoes, pruning tools, and mower blades.
- Add compost and top-dressing mulch to all unhealthy soil areas.
- Turn the compost pile regularly.
- Feed the birds!

---

* *Planting recommendations based on North Texas climate. Check with your local nurseries and extension service for specific varieties and timing in your area.*

MARCH

PLANT*:
- Trees and shrubs.
- Finish cool-season vegetable plantings. Begin warm-season crops after last killing freeze date.
- Plant a mixture of varieties and include some open-pollinated choices.
- Continue to plant cool-season annuals such as petunias and snapdragons. Begin planting warm-season types after last killing freeze.

FERTILIZE:
- All planting areas with a 100% organic fertilizer at approximately 20 lbs./1,000 sq. ft. (if not done in February).

PRUNE:
- Spring-flowering shrubs and vines only after they finish blooming: flowering quince, spirea, forsythia, weigela, azaleas, camellias, Carolina jessamine, wisteria, lady banksia rose, etc.
- Fruit trees just before bud break.

WATER:
- Annuals and other dry soil areas as needed.
- Wildflower areas in dry years.

PEST CONTROL:
- Loopers and caterpillars: *Bacillus thuringiensis* (Bt) biological worm spray.
- Pillbugs, snails, slugs: diatomaceous earth/garlic tea, beer traps, sabadilla.
- Aphids: soap and water or garlic tea. A blast of water and a release of ladybugs is even better.
- Black spot, powdery mildew, bacterial leaf spot: baking soda spray.
- Sycamore anthracnose: Bordeaux mixture as leaves emerge.
- Fruit tree sprays: garlic/pepper tea and baking soda. Start 2 weeks before bud break with the garlic/pepper tea. Spray the baking soda only as diseases appear. Spray fish emulsion and liquid seaweed every 2 weeks if time and budget allow.

ODD JOBS
- Turn the compost pile.
- Use completed compost for bed preparation—use partially completed compost as a top-dressing mulch.
- Mulch all bare soil.
- Feed the birds!

---

* *Planting recommendations based on North Texas climate. Check with your local nurseries and extension service for specific varieties and timing in your area.*

APRIL

PLANT*:
- Turfgrass from plugs, sod, sprigs, or seed.
- Roses from containers.
- Container-grown fruit and pecan trees.
- Warm-season flowers including: (sun) periwinkles, cosmos, portulaca, copper leaf, marigolds, zinnias, lantana; (shade) caladiums, coleus, begonias, impatiens, and nicotiana.
- Warm-season vegetables, including melons, okra, southern peas, corn, squash, beans, cucumbers, eggplant, and tomatoes.
- Summer/fall-flowering perennials.
- Herb-garden plants in beds, pots, and hanging baskets.

FERTILIZE:
- Summer-flowering shrubs and roses.
- Spray rose foliage with Epsom salts and garlic tea.
- Apply root stimulator monthly to newly planted trees and shrubs.
- Spray fish emulsion and seaweed on all foliage every 2 weeks.

PRUNE:
- Spring-blooming vines and shrubs immediately after bloom.
- Pick-prune hedges to be wider at the bottom for better light and thicker growth.

WATER:
- All planting areas deeply but infre-

quently during dry periods.
- Potted plants as needed.

PEST CONTROL:
- Release green lacewings for control of thrips in roses, glads, other flowers.
- Snails, slugs, pillbugs: diatomaceous earth and garlic/pepper tea, beer traps, or sabadilla.
- Release trichagromma wasps for pecan casebearers.
- Ticks, fleas, and chiggers: diatomaceous earth/pyrethrum products.
- Bacterial leaf spot of peaches and plums: Bordeaux mixture, baking-soda spray, or garlic/pepper tea.
- Aphids: water blast followed by release of ladybugs.
- Black spot on roses: baking-soda spray.
- Fire ants: Fire ant baits for large areas. Pour vinegar with diatomaceous earth or soapy water into individual mounds.

ODD JOBS:
- Mow weekly and leave clippings on the lawn.
- Turn compost pile.
- Continue to add new vegetative matter and manure to existing and additional compost piles.
- Mulch all bare soil.
- Feed the birds!

* *Planting recommendations based on North Texas climate. Check with your local nurseries and extension service for specific varieties and timing in your area.*

MAY

PLANT*:
- Lawn grasses from plugs, sod, seed, or sprigs or by hydromulching.
- Tropical color in beds or pots: bougainvillea, mandevilla, allamanda, penta, hibiscus, and others.
- Trees and shrubs.
- Warm-season annual color plants: lantana, begonia, zinnia, periwinkle, cosmos, verbena, and others.
- Cannas, glads, caladiums, and other summer bulbs. Mums and other fall perennials.
- Ground covers from 2¼" or 4" pots.
- Hot-weather vegetables, including southern peas, okra, and melons.

FERTILIZE:
- All annual flowers and potted plants with organic fertilizers. Spray fish emulsion and seaweed on all foliage every 2 weeks.

PRUNE:
- Climbing roses, after their bloom.
- Spring-flowering shrubs, vines, and trees after they have bloomed.
- "Pinch" away the growing tips of mums weekly.

WATER:
- All planting areas deeply but infrequently during dry periods.
- Potted plants regularly.

PEST CONTROL:
- Release trichogramma wasps for pecan casebearer and moth larvae.
- Fleas, ticks, and chiggers: diatomaceous earth/pyrethrum products.
- Cabbage loopers and other caterpillars: *Bacillus thuringiensis* (Bt).
- Aphids on tender, new growth: strong water blast, soap and water, or garlic/pepper tea.
- Release green lacewings and ladybugs.
- Lacebugs on azaleas, sycamores: Soap and water or garlic/pepper tea.
- Weeds: hand remove or use mechanical devices.

ODD JOBS:
- Mow weekly and leave clippings on the lawn.
- Turn compost pile and continue to add new ingredients.
- Mulch all bare soil.
- Feed the birds!

* *Planting recommendations based on North Texas climate. Check with your local nurseries and extension service for specific varieties and timing in your area.*

JUNE

PLANT*:
- All warm-season grasses: bermuda, zoysia, St. Augustine, buffalo.
- Summer annual color: portulaca, marigold, zinnia, periwinkle, lantana, copperleaf, amaranthus, cosmos, and verbena.
- Tropical color: bougainvilleas, hibiscus, pentas, allamandas, mandevillas, etc.
- Shrubs and trees.
- Fall tomatoes.

FERTILIZE:
- All planting areas with a 100% organic fertilizer. This should be the second major fertilization.
- Spray all plantings and lawns with fish emulsion, seaweed, and molasses every 2 weeks.
- Iron deficiency results in yellowed leaves with dark green veins on the youngest growth. Apply iron and sulfur products. Epsom-salts spray will also help. Use high-calcium lime for calcium deficiency.

PRUNE:
- Blackberries, to remove fruiting canes after harvest. Prune new canes to 3' in height to encourage side branching.
- Remove spent flowers from daisies, daylilies, cannas, and other summer flowers.
- Dead and damaged wood from trees, shrubs, as needed.

WATER:
- All planting areas deeply but infrequently during dry periods.
- Potted plants regularly. Daily waterings are needed for some plants.

PEST CONTROL:
- Spider mites: garlic/pepper tea or soap and water. Spray every 3 days for 9 days.
- Fleas, ticks, chiggers: diatomaceous earth/pyrethrum products.
- Bagworms: (Bt) *Bacillus thuringiensis.*
- Webworms in pecans, persimmons: Bt and include 1 teaspoon of liquid soap to improve penetration.
- Scale insects, including mealy bugs: summer-weight horticultural oil.
- Black spot on roses, mildew, and other fungi: baking-soda spray.
- Weeds: hand remove and work on improving soil health.
- Lacebugs, elm leaf beetles: pyrethrum, garlic/pepper tea, summer-weight horticultural oil.

ODD JOBS:
- Mow weekly and leave clippings on the lawn.
- Turn compost pile.
- Mulch all bare soil.
- Feed the birds!

* *Planting recommendations based on North Texas climate. Check with your local nurseries and extension service for specific varieties and timing in your area.*

JULY

PLANT*:
- Color for fall: marigolds, zinnias, celosia, Joseph's coat, and aster.
- Container-grown nursery stock.
- Warm-season lawn grasses.
- Tomatoes, peppers, melons, other warm-season vegetables for fall garden.

FERTILIZE:
- All planting areas with organic fertilizers, if not done in June.
- Use iron/sulfur products for iron deficiency. Use high-calcium lime for calcium deficiency.
- Spray fish emulsion/seaweed products on all foliage.

PRUNE:
- Roses, to encourage fall bloom.
- Dead or damaged limbs.
- Flowering plants, to remove spent flower heads and encourage new flower production.

WATER:
- All planting areas deeply but infrequently during dry periods.
- Outdoor container plants daily, others as needed.

PEST CONTROL:
- Chinch bugs: diatomaceous earth/pyrethrum products.
- Elm leaf beetles, lace bugs: pyrethrum or summer-weight horticultural oil.
- Spider mites: soap and water or garlic/pepper tea. Spray every 3 days for 9 days.
- Fire ants: stir diatomaceous earth into mounds.
- Fleas, ticks, chiggers, bermuda mites: diatomaceous earth/pyrethrum products or sulfur in alkaline soils.
- Webworms and bagworms: *Bacillus thuringiensis* (Bt) with 1 teaspoon soap per gallon. Spray at dusk.
- Leaf rollers: *Bacillus thuringiensis* (Bt).
- Scale insects on euonymus, hollies, camellias: Use summer-weight oil. Apply dormant oil during winter. Remove unadapted plants.
- Weeds: hand remove or use mechanical devices.

ODD JOBS:
- Mow weekly and leave clippings on the lawn.
- Turn compost pile, add new ingredients, and start new piles.
- Mulch all bare soil with partially completed compost or other coarse-textured material.
- Feed the birds!

* *Planting recommendations based on North Texas climate. Check with your local nurseries and extension service for specific varieties and timing in your area.*

AUGUST

PLANT*:
- Fall color such as mums, asters, marigolds, zinnias, and celosia.
- Fall-flowering bulbs such as spider lilies, fall crocus, and fall amaryllis.
- Finish fall vegetable plantings of beans, corn, cucumbers, melons, and squash.
- Cool-season vegetables, including broccoli, cauliflower, brussel sprouts, cabbage, spinach, potatoes, lettuce, carrots, beets, radishes, and English peas.
- Finish planting warm-season lawn grasses: buffalo, bermuda, St. Augustine, and zoysia.
- Wildflower seed.

FERTILIZE:
- Foliar-feed all planting beds and lawns with fish emulsion, seaweed, and molasses every 2 weeks.

PRUNE
- Trim spent flower stalks and blossoms of annuals and perennials to stimulate regrowth of stems and blooms.
- Remove dead and damaged wood from shrubs and trees.

WATER:
- Water deeply and as infrequently as possible. Your garden and landscape will usually need more water this month than any other.
- Potted plants and hanging baskets daily or as needed.

PEST CONTROL:
- Grubworms: good soil culture is the best control. Apply beneficial nematodes as needed.
- Chinch bugs: diatomaceous earth.
- Aphids: soap and water or garlic tea. Water blast and release of ladybugs.
- Fire ants: Fire ant control for large areas. Soapy water or D.E. for individual mounds.
- Chewing insects: diatomaceous earth/pyrethrum products.
- Cabbage loopers and other caterpillars: *Bacillus thuringiensis* (Bt).
- Borers in peaches, plums, and other trees: Rotenone/pyrethrum, mulch root system.
- Release beneficial insects if needed: praying mantids, ladybugs, green lacewings.

ODD JOBS:
- Mow weekly and leave clippings on the lawn.
- Turn compost pile.
- Feed the birds!

---

* *Planting recommendations based on North Texas climate. Check with your local nurseries and extension service for specific varieties and timing in your area.*

SEPTEMBER

PLANT*:
- Cool-season, leafy root crops such as carrots, beets, turnips, etc.
- Wildflower seeds.
- Finish warm-season lawn grass plantings by early September.
- Transplant established spring-flowering bulbs, iris, daylilies, daisies, and peonies.
- Perennials.
- Cool-season grasses.

FERTILIZE:
- All planting areas with a 100% organic fertilizer at approximately 10 lbs./1,000 sq. ft.
- Foliar-feed all planting areas and lawns with fish emulsion, seaweed, and molasses.

PRUNE:
- Root-prune wisterias that failed to bloom.
- Remove spent blooms of summer-flowering perennials.
- Remove surface tree roots if needed, but no more than 20% of root system per year.

WATER:
- Water deeply during dry spells.
- Potted plants and hanging baskets regularly.

PEST CONTROL:
- Brown patch in St. Augustine: baking soda spray.

- Webworms, tent caterpillars: *Bacillus thuringiensis* (Bt).
- Grubworms: beneficial nematodes.
- Cabbage loopers on broccoli, cauliflower, cabbage, Brussels sprouts: *Bacillus thuringiensis* (Bt).
- Aphids on tender, new fall growth: garlic tea or water blast followed by release of ladybugs.
- Fire ants: Bait for large areas. Soapy water or D.E. for individual mounds.
- Roses for black spot and powdery mildew: baking soda and seaweed sprayed on alternated weeks.
- Iron chlorosis (yellowed leaves, dark green veins, newest growth first): chelated iron, and sulfur. Epsom salts if magnesium is deficient.

ODD JOBS:
- Mow weekly and leave clippings on the lawn.
- Turn the compost pile.
- Feed the birds!

---

* Planting recommendations based on North Texas climate. Check with your local nurseries and extension service for specific varieties and timing in your area.

OCTOBER

PLANT*:
- Pansies, violas, pinks, snapdragons, flowering cabbage and kale, English daisies, Iceland poppies, wallflowers, and other cool-season flowers.
- Complete wildflower plantings.
- Trees, shrubs, vines, and spring- and summer-flowering perennials.
- Strawberries.
- Cool-season grasses.

FERTILIZE:
- Foliar-feed all plantings and lawns with fish emulsion, seaweed, and molasses. Test soil annually to monitor accumulations of phosphorous and balance of all minerals. Mulch all bare soil. Add new material to the top of all existing mulch where exposed.

WATER:
- Newly planted wildflower areas if no rain.
- Newly planted annuals.

PRUNE:
- Pick-prune shrubs as needed, but save major tree pruning for winter.
- Remove dead and damaged wood from trees.

PESTS:
- Brown patch in St. Augustine: baking-soda spray.
- Peach leaf curl: Bordeaux mixture or garlic/pepper tea.

- Cabbage loopers in garden: *Bacillus thuringiensis* (Bt).
- To reflower a poinsettia, give it uninterrupted darkness 14 hours each day and 10 hours of bright light each day until December. It's better to buy new plants each year.

ODD JOBS:
- Mow weekly and leave the clippings on the lawn.
- Build new compost piles and turn old ones.
- Use completed compost to prepare new planting beds.
- Use partially completed compost as a top-dressing mulch for ornamentals and vegetables.
- Feed the birds!

* *Planting recommendations based on North Texas climate. Check with your local nurseries and extension service for specific varieties and timing in your area.*

NOVEMBER

PLANT*:
- Trees and shrubs.
- Spring bulbs, including daffodils and grape hyacinths. Precool tulips and hyacinths for 45 days at 40° prior to planting.
- Spring- and summer-flowering perennials, including daisies, iris, daylilies, lilies, thrift, lythrum, etc.
- Spring-flowering annuals, including pansies, pinks, snapdragons, flowering cabbage and kale, English daises, California and Iceland poppies.
- Winter-hardy nursery stock.
- Cool-season grasses.

FERTILIZE:
- Bulbs, annuals, and perennials with earthworm castings and other gentle, organic fertilizers.
- Indoor plants with earthworm castings and other low-odor, organic fertilizers.

WATER:
- All planting areas at least once if no rain.

PRUNE:
- Begin major tree pruning. Remove dead limbs before leaves fall.
- Pick-prune shrubs to remove longest shoots if needed.
- Remove spent blooms and seed heads from flowering plants.
- Cut off tops of brown perennials. Leave roots in the soil.

PESTS:
- Watch roots of removed annuals for nematodes (knots on the roots). Treat infected soil with biostimulants, molasses, and compost.
- Watch houseplants for spider mites, scale, aphids. Spray as needed with biostimulants and mild soap and seaweed. Use light weight oils as a last resort.
- Watch lawn for signs of grubworm damage. Grass will be loose on top of ground. Treat with beneficial nematodes.

ODD JOBS:
- Have landscape and garden soils tested now to determine soil-balancing needs.
- Pick tomatoes the night before the first freeze. Let them ripen indoors.
- Put all fallen leaves, spent annuals, and other vegetative matter into the compost piles.
- Add mulch to your garden—do not cultivate once healthy soil has been developed.
- Mulch all bare ornamental beds for winter protection.
- Turn compost piles.
- Feed the birds!

* *Planting recommendations based on North Texas climate. Check with your local nurseries and extension service for specific varieties and timing in your area.*

DECEMBER

PLANT*:
- Trees and shrubs.
- Living Christmas trees (after use) that are adapted to the area's climate and soils.
- Spring bulbs, including tulips and hyacinths.

FERTILIZE:
- Greenhouse plants with organic fertilizers.
- Houseplants, once or twice during winter, with earthworm castings or other odorless organic fertilizers.

WATER:
- Any dry areas to help protect against winter cold injury.

PRUNE:
- Peaches, plums, and other fruit trees.
- Apples, to remove vertical shoots.
- Evergreens, to adjust the appearance.
- Shade trees to remove dead and damaged wood.
- Cut off tops of spent perennials. Leave roots in the ground.

PESTS:
- Bark aphids on trees: no treatment needed.
- Scale insects on shade and fruit trees: dormant oil if heavy infestation.
- Cut mistletoe out of trees. Remove infested limbs if possible.
- Spray houseplants with seaweed, mild soap, and biostimulants to control scale, mealy bugs, spider mites, and other insects.
- Remember that henbit, clover, and other wildflowers are beautiful, so don't worry about spraying them.

ODD JOBS:
- Pick tomatoes the night before first freeze.
- Clean and oil tools before storing for winter.
- Run mower, trimmer engines dry of gasoline. Drain and change oil. Take to repair shop now to avoid the spring rush.
- Mulch all bare soil.
- Turn compost piles.
- Feed the birds!

---

* Planting recommendations based on North Texas climate. Check with your local nurseries and extension service for specific varieties and timing in your area.

6

PEST CONTROL

PEST CONTROL

"The answer to pest problems is not in a bag of poisonous chemicals, but in a better understanding of the laws of nature and a desire to work with these laws."

Malcolm Beck, San Antonio 1988

E ver wondered how insects were kept under control or why plants weren't devoured by destructive insects before man started to "control" the environment? The answer lies in the fact that nature has a balanced, natural order.

With the proliferation of chemicals during the twentieth century, many beneficial insects have been killed along with the harmful insects. Generally, the harmful ones will re-establish themselves more quickly than will the beneficial ones, and plant loss accelerates. Encouraging the beneficial insects to be established again is a primary goal of an organic program. However, there are many safe or low-toxic products available to transition from a chemical program to an organic program that will reduce the harmful effects to beneficial insect population.

A report by the scientific journal *Bioscience* says that a mere 1% of the pesticides applied to plants ever reaches its ultimate destination—the insects. The other 99% pollute and poison the air, soil, water, good bugs, animals, and man.

This section is divided into two parts—one on harmful insects and one on beneficial insects. We will first discuss the beneficial insects and how they can help keep the harmful insects under control. After all, keeping them under control is all that is really needed, since the ones that are not killed will serve as a lure for the beneficial insects. We will then discuss the major harmful insects first, along with how to control them with biological and/or organic pesticides.

BENEFICIAL INSECTS

I t would be impossible to cover all the beneficial insects because somewhere around 98% of the world's insects are beneficial. It could be argued that even the destructive bugs are good because they eliminate weak plants.

Friendly bugs are being used more

and more to help control destructive insects in vegetable gardens, stored grain, greenhouses, and orchards. Parasitic mites and wasps are being used to control houseflies, barnyard flies, and fire ants.

Earthworms, centipedes, and millipedes are not technically insects, but they are beneficial, especially the earthworm. The centipedes and millipedes are helpful because they aerate the soil, produce nutrients, and help break down organic material.

A critical element of an organic program is the establishment and maintenance of biodiversity. That means the vegetable garden and landscaping need to have a healthy and dynamic mix of insects, plants, animals, and birds. Man needs to fit into that puzzle as well. Here's some information on the insects that can help you maintain your gardens.

The best way to control troublesome insects is to allow them to control themselves. Nature provides beautiful checks and balances if we allow them to function.

BENEFICIAL INSECTS

GROUND BEETLES

One-third of all animals and 40% of all insects are beetles. All beetles have hard, opaque wing covers that meet in a straight line down the middle of their backs. The ground beetles are important predators of plant-eating insects. They usually feed at night on soft-bodied larvae including cankerworms and tent caterpillars. They also eat many kinds of slugs and snails. Soldier beetles feed on aphids, grasshopper eggs, cucumber beetles, and various caterpillars.

LADYBUGS

Lady bird beetle is the proper term, but these little friends are best known as ladybugs. The ladybug is the most popular and most universally known beneficial insect. There are several hundred different kinds in North America and all are beneficial. The most common native varieties are the black with red spots and the gray with black spots. They are all very helpful and should be protected. The orange with black spots is the most available commercially.

larva

Yellow ladybug eggs are visible in the winter and early spring in clusters on the backs of leaves and on the trunks of trees. The adult ladybug can eat 200 aphids per day, the larvae 70-100 per day. The larvae and the adult beetles eat large quantities of aphids and other small, soft-bodied insects such as scale, thrips, and mealy bugs. They should be released after aphids are visible and at

pupa

Beneficial Insects Continued

night after the foliage has been wet down. Let a few out at a time to see if they are hungry. If they fly away, put them in the refrigerator for a day or two and try again later after they have used up their stored food. Ladybugs will store in the refrigerator for a few days (35-45° is best for storage). They will remain dormant and alive under these cool temperatures, although storage tends to dry them out and a few will die. They will naturalize if chemical sprays are eliminated.

For ladybugs to mature and lay eggs, they need a nectar and pollen source, such as flowering plants. Legumes such as peas, beans, clover, and alfalfa are especially good. To make an artificial food, dilute a little honey with a small amount of water and mix in a little brewer's yeast or bee pollen. Streak tiny amounts of this mixture on small pieces of waxed paper, and fasten these to plants. Replace these every 5-6 days, or when they become moldy. Keep any extra food refrigerated between feedings. The ladybug's favorite real food is the aphid.

If ladybugs are released indoors or in a greenhouse, you might want to screen off any openings to prevent their escape.

FIREFLIES (LIGHTNING BUGS)

The firefly is a fascinating insect that produces a light by releasing luciferin from its abdomen to combine with oxygen. When conditions are right the male

Beneficial Insects Continued

flashes his light every 6 seconds to be answered by the female 2 seconds later. Firefly larvae feed on snails, slugs, cutworms, and mites.

GREEN LACEWINGS

The green lacewing is a beautiful, fragile, light-green or brown insect with lustrous, yellow eyes. The adult is approximately 1/2" long, holds its wings up tentlike when at rest, and feeds on honeydew, nectar, and pollen. The adults really aren't terribly beneficial. They just fly around, look pretty, and mate. The larvae, on the other hand, are voracious eaters of aphids, red spider mites, thrips, mealybugs, cottony cushion scale, and many worms.

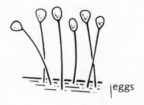

eggs

larva

cocoon

adult

The lacewing larvae (also known as "aphid lions") emerge from the eggs, which appear on the end of thin, white filaments attached to leaves or stems. The larva pupates by spinning a cocoon with silken thread. The adult emerges in about 5 days by cutting a hole in the cocoon.

If it is inconvenient to release the lacewing immediately after purchase, the eggs or larvae may be refrigerated for a few days, but be careful not to freeze. 38° to 45°F will delay development but not hurt the eggs.

Eggs and larvae can be hand sprinkled wherever harmful insects exist or are suspected. Even if you put them in the wrong place, they will search almost 100 feet for their first meal. One of the best ways to distribute lacewing

Beneficial Insects Continued

eggs and larvae is with a pill bottle with a small hole in the cap. A salt shaker will work but you have to increase the size of the holes. A thimble will hold about 10,000 eggs. Releasing the green lacewing from a card or cup mounted in a tree will keep the fire ants from getting them before they do their work. It helps to put a sticky material such as Tanglefoot™ on the trunk of the tree to block the ant's access.

Lacewing larvae are gray in color. They look like tiny alligators and mature in 2-3 weeks. Biweekly releases are ideal. Flowering plants attract green lacewings; buckwheat is especially good.

PREDATORY MITES

The adult predatory mite is orange in color. The immature stages are a pale salmon color. They can be differentiated from the "red" two-spotted spider mite by the lack of spots on either side. The body is pear-shaped, and the front legs are longer than those of pest mites. Predatory mites move about quickly when disturbed or exposed to bright light, and they multiply twice as quickly as pest mites do, with the females laying about 50 eggs. They eat from 5 to 20 eggs or mites per day.

Release predatory mites at the first sign of spider mite damage. For heavy infestations, you will probably need to reduce the populations of pest mites with organic sprays such as insecticidal soaps or garlic/pepper tea and seaweed.

Beneficial Insects Continued

PRAYING MANTIDS

These fierce looking but friendly critters will eat almost any insect, especially caterpillars, grasshoppers, beetles,
and other damaging pests. Be careful
not to confuse the egg cases with the
asp, which is a soft, hairy insect with a
powerful sting. The praying mantis egg
case looks very similar to an asp but is
hard like papier-mache. The only negative about praying mantids is that they
also eat beneficial insects. They don't
usually eat ladybugs, however, because
ladybugs are bitter.

SPIDERS

Most spiders are beneficial and harm-
less with the exceptions of the black
widow and brown recluse. You'll rarely
see a brown recluse because they seek
out dark corners in closets, etc., and
move about at night. The female black
widow is easy to identify by the red hour-
glass on her abdomen. Beware of her
because her venomous sting is very powerful and can cause illness and even
death. The puny little male isn't much
trouble; in fact, the female devours him
after mating.

WASPS

All wasps and mud daubers are beneficial. One of their favorite foods is the
tent caterpillar that often disfigures pecan trees. The tiny trichogramma wasp
is very effective for controlling cutworms, moths, and the pecan casebearer
by laying its eggs on the eggs of the

Beneficial Insects Continued

pests. When the wasp's eggs hatch, the larvae feed on the eggs of the pest. Wasps will sting only if you threaten them, and the mud dauber only if you grab it! Trichogramma and other friendly wasps don't sting at all. The mud dauber's favorite food is the black widow spider. It's also good for controlling flies in horse stables. Braconid wasps kill pests by laying their eggs in hosts like hornworms, codling moths, and aphids.

TRICHOGRAMMA WASPS

Trichogramma wasps or "moth egg parasites" are used to control pecan casebearer, cabbage worms, tomato horn worms, corn earworms, and other caterpillars. They are gnat-like parasitic wasps which attack over 200 types of worm pests. The trichogramma wasp stings the pest worm egg and deposits its own egg inside. The egg hatches and the larva feeds on and kills the pest.

Early application of trichogramma before a problem has been diagnosed is the ideal way to begin a pest control program. Weekly or biweekly releases throughout the early growing season are ideal.

WHITEFLY PARASITES

The whitefly parasite can help to deter serious damage to tomatoes, cucumbers, and ornamental plants. *Encarsia formosa* is a small, efficient parasite of the whitefly. It is about the size of a spider mite. It attacks the whitefly in the immature

Beneficial Insects Continued

stages, laying eggs in the third and fourth stages, while feeding off the first and second stages. Early application of *Encarsia formosa* prior to heavy infestations is recommended. Parasites should be released at the first sign of whitefly.

NEMATODES

Beneficial nematodes are microscopic roundworms used to control cutworms, armyworms, corn rootworms, cabbage loopers, Colorado potato beetles, grubworms, termites, and other soil pests.  Nematodes enter the insect pest through the mouth or other body openings. Once inside the host, the nematodes feed and reproduce until the food supply is gone. Then hordes of nematodes emerge in search of new victims. Sounds pretty gross, doesn't it? Early applications prior to heavy pest infestations, followed by monthly applications, are the ideal solution.

Heterorhabditis (Heteros) are best for grubs. Steinernema (Steiners) work for grubs but are better for moths. Other beneficial insects include syrphid flies, parasitodes, big-eyed bugs, pirate bugs, and many, many others.

And, of course, anyplace you use beneficial insects, you'll want to avoid spraying with pesticides.

SOURCES FOR BENEFICIAL BUGS*

Arbico, P.O. Box 4247, Tuscon, AZ 85738
1-800-827-2847

Biofac, P.O. Box 87, Mathis, TX 78368
(512) 547-3259

Bio Insect Control, 710 S. Columbia, Plainview, TX 79072
(806) 293-5861

Biome, P.O. Box 6706, Katy, TX 77491-7606
(800) 998-1701

Biosys, 1057 E. Meadow Circle, Palo Alto, CA 94303
(415) 856-9500

Integrated Pest Management, 305 Agostino Road, San Gabriel, CA 91776
(818) 287-1101

M & R Duranga, P.O. Box 886 Bayfield, Colorado 81122
(800) 526-4075

Mellinger's Nursery, 2310 W. South Range Road, North Lima, OH 44452
(800) 321-7444

Natural Gardening Research Ctr., P.O. Box 149, Sunman, IN 47041
(812) 623-3800

Nature's Control, P. O. Box 35, Medford, OR 97501
(503) 899-8318

Necessary Trading Co., P.O. Box 603, New Castle, VA 24127
(703) 864-5103

OrCon, Inc., 5132 Venice Blvd., Los Angeles, CA 90019
(213) 937-7444

Organic Pest Management, P.O. Box 55267, Seattle, WA 98155
(206) 367-7007

Pest Management Services, Rt. 12, Box 346-31, Lubbock, TX 79424,
(806) 794-6761

Rincon-Vitova Insectaries, P.O. Box 95, Oak View, CA 93022
(800) 248-BUGS

Best source: Your local neighborhood nursery or feed store.

HARMFUL INSECTS

APHIDS

Aphids are sucking insects that can destroy the tender growth of plants, causing stunted and curled leaf growth and leaving a honeydew deposit. They can be controlled by using biodegradable soap and water or fish emulsion or just strong blasts of water. They are the favorite food of green lacewings and ladybugs. Protecting ladybugs and lacewings and promoting soil health and biodiversity is the best control for these indicator pests. Regular releases of beneficial insects give excellent control, but adapted plants and healthy soil is the best permanent control.

ANTS

There are many different ants, including carpenter ants, fire ants, and pharaoh ants. Solutions for ants indoors include diatomaceous earth, boric acid, diacide, and pyrethrum. Pyrethrum is effective and safe on ants indoors. Baits are very effective for large-scale infestations of fire ants. Vinegar or garlic tea poured directly on the mound also seems to work quite well. Both liquids work better if $1/4$ cup of diatomaceous earth is added to each gallon of liquid. Pyrethrum/rotenone products are excellent for knocking out individual mounds. Soapy water poured into individual mounds is a safe and effective technique.

Harmful Insects Continued

BAGWORMS

Bagworms are a common pest of ornamental trees and some shrubs. They will prey on many different species of plants such as cedar, juniper, cypress, etc. In the larval stage they can defoliate trees. They can be controlled by *Bacillus thuringiensis* (Bt). Hand picking the bags is also beneficial for control. Trichogramma wasps can help to control problem infestations.

BEES

Bees are beneficial and should be protected. For the proper environmental control, contact the beekeeper club or society in your area. They will usually come and get them or give you advice on control. Problem bees can be killed with soapy water.

BEETLES

Many adult beetles eat plant foliage and can destroy plants completely. An effective solution for destructive beetles is dry diatomaceous earth and sabadilla. Garlic tea is an even less toxic control. It's important to remember that many beetles are beneficial and only eat problem insects.

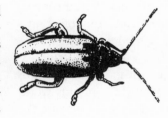

BORERS

Borers attack softwood trees and trees in stress. Adult beetles will eat tender terminal growth and then deposit their eggs in the base of the tree. Eggs hatch into larvae and bore into trees and tunnel through the wood until the tree is

Harmful Insects Continued

weakened. Active, tunneling larvae can be killed with a stiff wire run into the holes. Rotenone™ and pyrethrum applied full strength directly in holes with putty to seal in the fumes will usually kill active larvae, but keeping trees healthy and out of stress is the best prevention. Quinine placed in holes will also work. Nicotine sulfate will also work but is very dangerous to handle. A generous amount of diatomaceous earth at the base of susceptible trees will also help.

CABBAGE LOOPERS
Cabbage loopers are the larvae of moths that are brown with silver spots in the middle of each wing. They can be killed with Bt spray when the insects are young. Use soap as a surfactant and spray late in the day since these guys feed at night. Trichogramma wasps will also help control these critters. It's interesting that even the chemical "pushers" admit that the chemical insecticides are ineffective at controlling loopers..

CANKERWORMS
The canker worm hangs on a silk thread from trees. He or she doesn't do a lot of damage. Wasps will usually control them. If not, use Bt for heavy infestations.

CATERPILLARS
Caterpillars are best known for their ability to defoliate trees and veggies. *Bacillus thuringiensis* (Bt) is an excellent

Harmful Insects Continued

biological control. Wasps are also a great help in controlling caterpillars of all kinds. Remember that caterpillars grow up to be beautiful butterflies, so don't kill them all.

CHIGGERS

Chiggers are known for their very annoying bite. The itching usually starts the day after you are bitten and lasts 2 to 4 days. Diatomaceous earth and sulfur will help prevent bites and control the critters. Vinegar rubbed on bites will eliminate the itching.

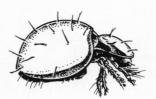

CHINCH BUGS

Chinch bugs are tiny, black, pinhead-size or smaller bugs. During hot, dry weather, chinch bugs can destroy unhealthy lawns. The lawns will look yellow, turn brown, and then die. A solution is diatomaceous earth or a pyrethrum/rotenone product. This insect hardly ever attacks healthy, well-maintained grass.

CRICKETS

Crickets live in and out of doors, destroy fabrics such as wool, cotton, synthetics, and silk, and also attack plants. Their irritating sound is the primary objection, although they will eat tender sprouts of wildflowers and vegetables. Solutions include diatomaceous earth, pyrethrum, and rotenone outdoors, and boric acid for indoor use. *Nosema locustae* is the best overall control available.

Harmful Insects Continued

ELM LEAF BEETLES

Wherever there is an American, Siberian, or cedar elm tree, the elm leaf beetle can be found. The elm leaf beetle will eat and damage lots of foliage and then move to the next tree. Trees can die from defoliation but only unhealthy trees are seriously attacked by elm leaf beetles. Solutions include diatomaceous earth, soap spray, and fish emulsion/seaweed. Strong populations of beneficial insects will also help.

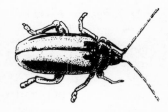

FIRE ANTS

Field tests by the Texas Department of Agriculture have shown that Logic™ fire ant bait, also sold as Award™, can provide control for an entire year, while the other bait products may need to be reapplied in late summer or fall. Although Logic™ may provide the longest control, it is also the slowest to take effect, requiring several weeks to completely eliminate colonies. The active ingredient, fenoxycarb, is an insect growth regulator that interferes with egg laying by the queens and prevents the maturing of young ants. It does not kill the adult ants, however, which live out their normal life spans. The colony is slowly eliminated by attrition.

Individual mounds can be killed out by stirring dry diatomaceous earth into the hills. If pyrethrum is added to the mix, it works even better. The D.E. treatment is not effective on humid days. By the way, dry instant grits poured on top of mounds also works.

Harmful Insects Continued

FLEAS

Fleas are nasty little things and it's curious why they were created. Fleas can live for many months without food. They generally invade a house by a pet or on people. While not destructive to plants, they are a nuisance for pets and their owners. Control with diatomaceous earth and pyrethrum dusted or sprayed around pets' favorite resting spots. Insect growth regulators such as Precor™ or other methoprene products are a helpful control of problem infestations inside the house. Bathing the pets regularly with mild soapy water is good and feeding the pets a balanced, organic diet is important, as is exercise. Supplement pet food with diatomaceous earth, garlic, and food grade kelp. Brewers yeast sometimes helps as well. Plant rue, wormwood, and pennyroyal mint. Other controls are Demize™ for indoors and pyrethrum/rotenone for outdoors.

FLIES

Flies can be repelled with fresh, crushed tansy or garlic. They can also be killed with fly swatters. On the farm they can be greatly reduced by feeding the animals small amounts of diatomaceous earth. Fly parasites are the most economical and most effective control.

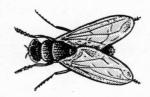

FLEAHOPPERS

This is a common vegetable-garden pest. It sucks juices from the foliage and causes a loss of leaf color which stresses plants. Sulfur and diatomaceous earth will usually get rid of them.

Harmful Insects Continued

FOREST TENT CATERPILLARS

These caterpillars will sometimes do some damage in early spring, but if pesticides are avoided, the beneficial wasps will usually keep these guys under control. Bt can be used if they get out of hand. At worst they are only a temporary problem.

FUNGUS GNATS

Fungus gnats are present when the soil surface is too wet. They do little, if any, damage but are annoying. They can be gotten rid of by drying out the soil. Baking soda sprayed lightly on soil will quickly solve the problem.

GRASSHOPPERS

Grasshoppers feed on numerous plants. They are usually kept in check by natural predators such as birds, but on occasion the conditions can be right for them to increase to numbers significant enough to be devastating. They can be controlled by sabadilla dust or pyrethrum/rotenone mix. A soap spray will help by making the foliage less tasty. Garlic/pepper tea will also discourage them. *Nosema locustae* is an effective, long-term, biological control.

GRUBWORMS

Adult June beetles will chew leaves, and subterranean grubs will eat roots of grass and garden plants. Solutions include milky spore disease and beneficial nematodes. Some experts say that milky spore disease will not control white grubs, but many organic gardeners say that it will.

Harmful Insects Continued

You be the judge. Grubs are rarely a problem in healthy, biologically active, well-drained soil.

LACEBUGS

Lacebugs attack various deciduous trees and broad-leafed evergreens. The lacebug is flat and oval and sucks the sap from the underside of the leaf. A quick solution for this pest is garlic/pepper tea and diatomaceous earth, or sabadilla. Healthy biodiversity in the garden will eliminate a destructive population of this pest.

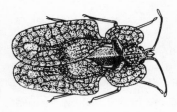

LEAFHOPPERS

Leafhoppers excrete honeydew and damage leaves by stripping them, causing stunted, dwarfed, and yellow foliage. They can be controlled with pyrethrum or simply by the encouragement of diverse populations of beneficial insects.

LEAF MINERS

Leaf miners will cause brown foliage tips which often continue over the entire leaf. Neem products are effective. A fish emulsion/seaweed mix will help. They cause minor damage only, so treatment is rarely needed.

LEAF SKELETONIZERS

Same as sawfly caterpillar. Does cosmetic damage to red oak and other tree leaves. Not usually necessary to treat. Damage is usually confined to isolated spots in the foliage.

Harmful Insects Continued

MEALYBUGS

Mealybugs are sucking insects that look like cotton on plant stems. Mealybugs suck sap from the foliage and stems and can destroy plants. Mealybugs like warm weather and also infest houseplants. Helpful controls include soap and water, predator insects, diatomaceous earth, and lizards. For houseplant problems, dab alcohol on bugs with a cotton swab.

MOSQUITOS

A liquid spray containing vitamin B complex is helpful. Solutions are to overturn any object that can hold water and not let water stand or collect. There are other solutions such as pyrethrum, purple martins, frogs, toads, and bats. *Bacillus thuringiensis* 'Israelensis' will kill mosquitos in decorative ponds without harming fish or aquatic plants. Encouraging birds, especially purple martins, is extremely helpful. Bats are also great friends in controlling mosquitos. Garlic/pepper tea can be sprayed before a party or outdoor event to lessen the problem. Citronella candles will also help to repel these miserable pests.

NEMATODES

Many nematodes are beneficial, but there are those that will attack ornamental trees, garden plants, and lawn grass. Controls include increasing the organic level in soil, using organic fer-

Harmful Insects Continued

tilizers, and applying products that increase microbial activity. Cedar flakes
applied to the soil surface will also help.
Beneficial nematode products are also
very helpful.

PILL BUGS

Pill bugs, sow bugs, or roly-poly bugs
are crustaceans and related to shrimp,
crabs, and crawfish. They are found in
damp places and feed on organic matter but when abundant will also eat
plants. Solutions include 5% rotenone
and sabadilla. Beer in a trap is still one
of the best solutions. Banana peels attract them so you can scoop them up
and drop into a soapy water solution.

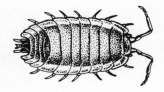

PLUM CURCULIOS

Rotenone/pyrethrum, applied when
75% of the flower petals have fallen, is
the organic version of the extension service control. It's a waste of time but you
can do it if you want to. Thick mulch,
at least 4" of compost, rough bark, or
tree chips is important. Regular spraying of garlic tea is the best organic preventative. Biodiversity is critical for control of this pest. Spray foliage biweekly
with fish emulsion and seaweed.

RED SPIDER MITES

Red spider mites are very small and feed
on garden plants and ornamental trees.
You probably will not see the mites but
you will notice the webbing that ac-
companies them. The best control is

Harmful Insects Continued

beneficial insects such as green lacewing. Controls also include spraying water or garlic/pepper tea on the underside of the infected leaves every 3 days
for 9 days. Strong blasts of water or soapy
water are good for small infestations.
Predatory mites are also effective.

ROACHES

There are numerous cockroaches, but
only a few really pose a problem. Cockroaches usually live out of doors and are
nocturnal by nature. Roaches will enter a home or building through any crack
or crevice. They will chew on cloth or
books. Some solutions are a shoe, newspaper, diatomaceous earth, keeping your
house clean, eliminating standing water, and sealing all openings. Boric acid
indoors gives effective control. Silica
gel is also good. Eliminating the food
and water sources is a great help. To
make boric balls, mix 1 cup boric acid,
1 cup flour, $^{1}/_{2}$ cup sugar, and water.
Roll into cakes and place behind appliances out of the reach of pets and children.

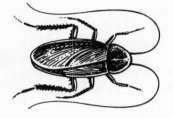

SCALE

Scale insects attach to stems, branches,
and trunks and suck sap from the plants.
Controls include lime sulfur spray, pyrethrum, horticultural oil, and dormant
oil. Use soap and water with seaweed
on interior plants. The black, scale-eat-
ing ladybug is very helpful.

Harmful Insects Continued

SLUGS

Slugs and snails must be kept moist at all times and will go anywhere there is moisture. I hate these little slime balls! Effective controls include garlic tea and diatomaceous earth, beer traps, sabadilla, and wood ashes.

SQUASH BUGS

Squash bugs are difficult-to-control bugs that attack squash, cucumbers, pumpkins, and other cucurbits. Control by smashing the eggs, dusting the adults with sabadilla, and planting lemon balm in between plants. Dusting young plants regularly with cheap self-rising flour will also help.

SQUASH VINE BORERS

The squash vine borer is an insect whose larva is a worm that bores into the base stem of squash, cucumber, melon, gourd, and pumpkin. Controls: cut the stem open, remove the worms, and cover the wounded area with soil. Another way is to inject Bt into the base of the stem with a syringe. Spraying with Bt will also help.

STINK BUGS

Stink bugs sting fruit and cause rotted spots. Some stink bugs are beneficial. They can be controlled with sabadilla.

TERMITES

Timbor™ is a boric-acid wood-treatment product that is effective. Using a 16-grit-sand barrier on the inside and outside of grade beams works well. New

Harmful Insects Continued

construction can use the sand under the slab. Pyrethrum/rotenone will kill the pests on contact. Boric acid and sulfur on top of the soil will also help.

THRIPS

Thrips attack the buds and tight-petaled flowers such as roses, mums, and peonies. Thrips are not visible to the naked eye but will rasp the plant tissue and drain the sap. When there is an infestation, they can kill a plant. Thrips are general eaters and will attack flowers or field crops. Controls include liquid kelp, pyrethrum, and green lacewings. Nicotine sulfate can be used as a last resort. Biweekly spraying of fish emulsion and seaweed is all that is usually needed.

TICKS

Ticks are difficult to control, but the diatomaceous earth/pyrethrum/rotenone sprays work quite well. Bathing the pets regularly will help considerably.

WHITEFLIES

Whiteflies are very small and resemble little white moths. Whiteflies are extremely hard to control with chemicals and will suck the juices from several kinds of plants. They will attack vegetables and ornamental plants outdoors and indoors. Seaweed and garlic/pepper tea spray have been my most effective controls for infestations. However, beneficial insect populations will prevent the pest. White flies have many natural enemies.

ORGANIC PEST REMEDIES

APHIDS

Controls	Application
Water blast	Use hose nozzle or a strong thumb.
Soap and water	1 tsp. per gal.
Garlic/pepper tea	Spray as needed.
Beneficial insects	Release ladybugs, braconid wasps, and green lacewings until a balanced population of bugs exists.

ANTS (Fire Ants, Carpenter Ants, and Pharoah Ants [Sugar])

Controls	Application
Baits	Apply on dry soil when ants are foraging.
Vinegar, garlic tea, hot water,	$1/4$ gallon poured in center of mound. Mix $1/4$ cup of diatomaceous earth into liquid for extra strength.
Boric Acid and sugar	Use in bait stations.
Pyrethrum	Dust problem areas.
Tansy	Sprinkle bits of tansy leaf in problem area.

BAGWORMS, CATERPILLARS, CORN BORERS, CABBAGEWORMS, ARMYWORMS

Controls	Application
Bt (Bacillus thuringiensis)	Spray with 1 tsp. soap per gal. at dusk.
Beneficial insects	Encourage and protect native wasps. Release green lacewings and trichogramma wasps.

BEETLES (Elm leaf beetle, Flea beetle, and Borer beetle)

Controls	Application
Pyrethrum	Make sure beetle in question is harmful—many are
Rotenone	beneficial.
Sabadilla	Encourage biodiversity of insects, birds, plants, and small animals.
	Use all per label instructions.

BORERS, TREE

Controls	Application
Pyrethrum/rotenone	Run stiff wire into borer holes.
Rotenone	Put insecticide into holes full strength and seal holes
Sabadilla	with putty.
	Mulch root system area of trees.

CASEBEARERS

Controls	Application
Trichogramma wasp	Release eggs at least every 2 weeks starting with first warm weather, usually mid-March.

CRICKETS, CHIGGERS, CHINCH BUGS

Controls	Application
Diatomaceous earth	Dust infested area @ 1 cup/1,000 sq.ft.
Pyrethrum	Per label instructions.
Mix the above	Mix with water at 2 tbs./gal. and spray infested area.
Nosema locustae (crickets—outside)	Broadcast on infested area.
Dusting sulfur (outside use)	Dust on legs to prevent chigger bites.

COLORADO POTATO BUG

Controls	Application
Bt/'San Diego'	Spray late in the day per label instructions.
Garlic/pepper tea and diatomaceous earth	Spray liquid mix as needed.

CUTWORMS

Controls	Application
Diatomaceous earth	Pour a ring of material around each plant.
Bone meal	Pour a ring of material around each plant.
Bt (Bacillus thuringiensis)	Apply per label at dusk. Add 1 tsp. soap per gal.
Collars	Wrap aluminum foil around veggie stem.

ELM LEAF BEETLE

Controls	Application
Insecticidal soap	1 tsp. per gallon.
Horticulture oil	Spray per label for severe problems.
Garlic tea with vegetable oil	1/4 cup concentrate per gallon.
Bt (Bacillus thuringiensis)	Spray per label at dusk.
Diatomaceous earth/pyrethrum products	Per label instructions.

FLIES

Controls	Application
Garlic tea	Spray infested area.
Yellow sticky traps	Hang in infested area.
Tansy	Grind the herb and apply as a dry powder.
Diatomaceous earth	Feed to livestock and pets with food.
Fly parasites	Release as needed.

FLEA BEETLES

Controls	Application
Rotenone/pyrethrum	Spray as needed on heavy infestations.
Garlic tea/diatomaceous earth	Spray at first sign of problem.

FLEAS

Controls	Application
Pyrethrum/rotenone products	Spray as needed.
Demize™ and Precor™ (indoors)	Label instructions.
Diatomaceous earth/pyrethrum	2 tsp. per gal. Spray infested area. 1 tsp. soap.
products (outdoors)	Bathe pets regularly in mild soapy water.

FUNGUS GNATS

Controls	Application
Baking soda spray	Spray lightly on soil.
Gnatol™	Apply per label instructions.
Water schedule	Allow soil to dry out.

GRASSHOPPERS

Controls	Application
Nosema locustae products	Broadcast per label instructions.
Hot pepper spray	Blast them as needed.

GRUBWORMS

Controls	Application
Beneficial nematodes	Release per label instructions.
All products that stimulate soil biology	Compost, organic fertilizers, microbial stimulators.
Snuff	Dust infested area with organic tobacco.

LACEBUGS

Controls	Application
Garlic/pepper tea	Spray liquid mix as needed.
Insecticidal soap	1 tsp./gal.
Horticultural oil	Per label instructions.
Pyrethrum/rotenone mix	Label instructions.
Beneficial insects	Release praying mantids and ladybugs as necessary.

LEAFHOPPERS

Controls	Application
Garlic/pepper tea plus diatomaceous earth	1/4 cup/gal. as needed.
Pyrethrum/rotenone products	Label instructions.
Praying mantids	Release as necessary.

LEAFMINERS

Controls	Application
Neem	Label instructions.
Don't worry about 'em	Minor damage only, usually no need to treat.

LOOPERS

Controls	Application
Bt (*Bacillus thuringiensis*)	Apply per label instructions at dusk.
Beneficial insects	Release regularly until healthy, native populations exist.

MEALYBUGS

Controls	Application
Horticulture oil	Label instructions.
Mealybug predators	Release as needed.
Lizards	Protect native ones and introduce new ones.

MITES

Controls	Application
Garlic/pepper tea	1/4 cup/gal. Spray every 3 days for 9 days.
Seaweed and soap spray	1 tbs/gal. Add 2 tsp. fish emulsion for extra effect.
Horticultural oil	Per label instructions.
Beneficial insects	Release green lacewings and predatory mites every two weeks while infestations exist.

MOSQUITOES

Controls	Application
Bti (*Bacillus thuringiensis* 'Israelensis')	Put briquettes in standing water.
Encourage frogs, birds, bats	Eliminate standing, stagnant water.
Instant coffee	Sprinkle crystals in standing water.
Garlic oil	Apply top standing water.
Gambusia and gold fish	Small fish that love the taste of mosquitoes.

MOTHS

Controls	Application
Bt (*Bacillus thuringiensis*)	Spray per label instructions at dusk.
Beneficial insects	Release ladybugs and green lacewings every two weeks until natural control exists.

NEMATODES

Controls	Application
Beneficial nematodes	Label instructions.
Organic matter	Stimulate soil biology with compost, organic fertilizers, and microbe stimulators.
Molasses	Apply dry material at 20 lbs./1,000 sq. ft.

PECAN CASE BEARER

Controls	Application
Trichogramma wasps	Release every 2 weeks during the spring. Start in mid-March or during first warm spell.
Green lacewings	Spray in early May.
BT (Bacilus Thurigiensis)	Spray in early May.

PILL BUGS (Sow bugs)

Controls	Application
Beer traps	Beer into a recessed plastic ice tea glass, jar, or dish.
Brewer's yeast and water traps	1 tablespoon of yeast per gallon of water.
Bone meal or colloidal phosphate	Pour a ring around each plant.
Diatomaceous earth or wood ashes	Pour a ring around each plant.

PLUM CURCULIO

Controls	Application
Pyrethrum/rotenone	Spray during petal fall.
Garlic/pepper tea	Spray during petal fall.
Mulch the tree's root system	Compost, shredded hardwood, or hay.

ROACHES

Controls	Application
Diatomaceous earth	Dust infested area lightly.
Boric acid	Dust infested areas lightly (indoors only).
Boric balls	Boric acid, flour, and sugar. Add water and roll in balls.
Sugar and baking-soda detergent traps	1-2 tablespoons per bait station.
Eliminate food source	Remove food and water sources daily.

SCALE

Controls	Application
Dormant oil	Label instructions in winter.
Horticultural oil	Per label instructions.
Beneficial insects	Release ladybugs and praying mantids.

SQUASH BUGS

Controls	Application
Sabadilla	Per label on serious infestations.
Hand removal	Destroy the metallic eggs from the back side of leaves.
Bee balm (lemon balm)	Interplant with veggies.

SQUASH VINE BORER

Controls	Application
Bt *(Bacillus thuringiensis)*	Spray very young plants and inject into stem with syringe.
Beneficial insects	Release trichogramma wasp and green lacewing.

STINK BUGS

Controls	Application
Sabadilla dust	Per label instructions as needed.
Garlic pepper tea/diatomaceous earth	$1/4$ cup per gallon of water as needed.

SLUGS, SNAILS

Controls	Application
Beer or brewer's yeast traps	Plastic jar or dish sunk into ground.
Garlic/pepper tea and Diatomaceous earth	Spray as needed.
Diatomaceous earth	Dust infested area.
Bone meal or colloidal phosphate	Dust infested area or put ring around individual plants.
Encourage turtles	The real life kind.

SPIDERS

Controls	Application
Physically remove	No need to control spiders except black widow and brown recluse.
Encourage	Most are beneficial.
Pyrethrum	Label instructions.

SOW BUGS (Pill bugs)

Controls	Application
Beer or brewer's yeast traps	Pour cheap beer into a recessed plastic iced tea glass, jar, or dish.
Bone meal, colloidal phosphate	Pour a ring around each plant.
Diatomaceous earth or wood ashes	Pour a ring around each plant.
Self-rising flour	Dust around infested plants.

SPIDER MITES

Controls	Application
Beneficial insects	Release green lacewings and predatory mites.
Liquid seaweed	2 tbs./gal. Add fish emulsion for extra effect.
Garlic/pepper tea	Spray every 3 days for 9 days.
Horticultural oil	Per label instructions. Last resort only.

TERMITES

Controls	Application
Sand barrier	16-grit (00 sand blasting) sand placed on both sides of the grade beam or under the slab.
Boric acid	Label instructions.
Nematodes	Apply to soil as preventative.
Rotenone/pyrethrum	Spray on active infestations.

TICKS

Controls	Application
Diatomaceous earth	2 tbs./gal. Spray or dust infected area.
Pyrethrum	1 tbs./gal. Spray infected area.
Mix of the two	2 tbs./gal. Spray infected area.
Pyrethrum/rotenone mix	2 tbs./gal. Spray infected area.

THRIPS

Controls	Application
Beneficial insects	Release green lacewing as needed.
Garlic/pepper tea	Spray every 2 weeks or as needed.

TOBACCO HORN WORM

Controls	Application
Bt (*Bacillus thuringiensis*)	Label instructions, at dusk.
Beneficial insects	Release trichogramma and braconid wasps every 2 weeks.

TOMATO PIN WORM

Controls	Application
Garlic/pepper tea	Spray every 2 weeks.
Pyrethrum/rotenone products	Spray as needed.

TREEHOPPERS

Controls	Application
Pyrethrum/rotenone	Spray for serious infestations per label instructions.
Garlic/pepper tea	Spray every 2 weeks or as needed.

WASPS

Controls	Application
Water blast (Protect if possible)	Nests can be moved to new location and nailed in place after spraying wasps with water. Do not attempt if allergic to wasps.

WHITEFLIES

Controls	Application
Garlic/pepper tea with seaweed	Spray as needed, weekly is best schedule.
Mineral oil/or vegetable oil	1 tsp./gal. Spray for severe infestations.
Yellow sticky traps	Hang in infested area.
Beneficial insects	Release until natural populations exist.

WEBWORMS

Controls	Application
Insecticidal soap	1 tsp. per gal. with diatomaceous earth.
Bt (*Bacillus thuringiensis*)	Spray with 1 tsp. soap per gal. at dusk.
Wasps	Introduce and protect trichogramma wasps and natives.

DISEASES

ORGANIC DISEASE CONTROL

Disease control in an organic program is an interesting situation. Increased resistance to most diseases results as a nice side benefit from the use of organic products, especially those containing the cytokinin-type hormones. Products in this catagory include Bioform™, Medina™, Agri Gro™, seaweed, Agrispon™, and others. These products are root growth stimulators and help to control all sorts of pathogens through increased biological activity.

All organic products help control disease to some degree. When soil is healthy, there is a never-ending microscopic war being waged between the good and bad microorganisms, and the good guys usually win. Disease problems are simply situations where the microorganisms have gotten out of balance. If allowed to do so, the good guys will control the bad guys.

Drainage is also a key ingredient for the prevention of diseases. Beds or tree pits that hold water and don't drain properly are the ideal breeding place for many disease organisms.

As with insects, spraying for diseases is only treating symptoms, not the major problems. The primary cause of problems is usually related to the soil and the root system. Therefore it is critical to improve drainage, increase air circulation, add organic material, and stimulate and protect the living organisms in the soil.

ANTHRACNOSE: A serious fungal problem in sycamore trees, beans, and ornamentals where the foliage turns a tan color overnight. Control is difficult other than by avoiding susceptable plants. Bordeaux or baking soda sprayed as leaves emerge in the spring will sometimes help. Best cure is soil improvement.

BACTERIAL BLIGHT: A bacterial disease that causes dark-green water spots that turn brown and may die leaving a hole in the leaves of tomatoes, plums, and several ornamental plants. Control includes healthy soil, baking-soda spray, garlic tea, and Bordeaux mix.

BLACK SPOT: More common name of fungal leaf spot. Black spot attacks the foliage of plants such as roses. There is usually a yellow halo around the dark spot. Entire leaves then turn yellow and ultimately die. Best controls include selection of resistant plants and baking-soda spray.

BROWN PATCH: Cool-weather, fungal disease of St. Augustine. Brown leaves pull loose easily from the runners. Small spots in lawn grow into large circles that look bad and weaken the turf but rarely kill the grass. Baking-soda spray is the best curative; soil health, drainage, and low nitrogen input are the best preventatives.

CANKER: A stress related disease of trees and shrubs that causes decay of the bark and wood. Healthy soil and plants are the best solution.

COTTON ROOT ROT: A fungal disease common in alkaline soils that attacks poorly adapted plants. The best preventative is healthy soil with a balance of nutrients and soil biology. Solutions include adding sulfur and sometimes sodium to the soil.

DAMPING OFF: Disease of emerging seedlings where tiny plants fall over as if severed at the ground line. Avoid by using living (not sterilized) soil and by placing colloidal phosphate on the surface of planting media.

ENTOMOSPORIUM: A disease of photinia and other plants that can be controlled by improving soil conditions and avoiding susceptible plants.

FIREBLIGHT: Disease of plants in the rose family where twigs and limbs die back as though they've been burned. Leaves usually remain attached but often turn black or dark brown. Prune back into healthy tissue and disinfect pruning tools with 3% solution of hydrogen peroxide. Spray plants at first sign of disease with Triple Action 20™.

GRAY LEAF SPOT: A disease of St. Augustine grass that forms gray vertical spots on the grass blades. A light baking-soda spray is the best curative. Prevent by improving soil health.

OAK WILT: A disease of the vascular system of oak trees which is transmitted through the air by insects and through the root system of neighboring trees by natural grafting. Biodiversity and soil health are the best deterrents.

POWDERY MILDEW: White or gray, powdery, fungal growth on the leaf surface and flower buds of zinnias, crape myrtles, and many vegetables. Best control is baking-soda spray.

SOOTY MOLD: Black fungal growth on the foliage of gardenias, crape myrtles, and other plants infested with aphids, scale, or whiteflies. It is caused by the honeydew (poop) of the insect pests. Best control is to release beneficial insects to control the pest bugs.

ST. AUGUSTINE DECLINE: Virus in common St. Augustine grass that causes a yellow mottling. The grass slowly dies away. The answer is to replace turf with a healthier grass. The best St. Augustine at the moment is "Raleigh."

ORGANIC DISEASE CONTROL

ANTHRACNOSE

Controls	Application
Liquid copper or Bordeaux mix	Spray per label on new foliage in early spring.
Baking-soda spray	Spray emerging foliage @ 4 teaspoons per gal.
Better soil health	Use mulch, compost, rock powders, biostimulants.

BACTERIAL BLIGHT

Controls	Application
Baking-soda spray	Spray lightly as needed.
Garlic/pepper tea	Spray as needed.
Better soil health	Use mulch, compost, rock powders, biostimulants.

BLACK SPOT (Fungal leaf spot)

Controls	Application
Lime-sulfur spray	Use label directions.
Baking-soda spray	Spray lightly as needed.
Liquid copper or Bordeaux mix	Spray as needed.
Better soil health	Use mulch, compost, rock powders, biostimulants.

BROWN PATCH

Controls	Application
Baking soda spray	Spray lightly as needed.
Better soil health	Mulch, compost, microbials, rock powders, biostimulants.
	Avoid wet soil and high- nitrogen fertilizer in late summer.

CANKER

Controls	Application
Increase drainage	Change planting site, aerate soil, mulch.
Delay pruning until bud swell	Never use flush cuts or pruning paint.
Paint tree trunks (fruit trees)	Paint tree trunks with white latex whitewash.
Better soil health	Mulch, compost, rock powders, biostimulantsœ.

FIREBLIGHT

Controls	Application
Garlic/pepper tea	Spray plants while in bloom.
Better soil health	Mulch, compost, rock powders, biostimulants.
Limit use of nitrogen	Cut off infected area.
Triple Action 20	Spray as needed.

GRAY LEAF SPOT

Controls	Application
Baking soda spray	Light foliage spray as needed.
Better soil health	Aerate and balance the soil nutrients.

OAK WILT

Controls	Application
Maintain soil and plant health	Fertilize with organic techniques, and water regularly.
Alamo™	Inject per instructions as a last resort.

POWDERY MILDEW

Controls	Application
Baking-soda spray	Light foliage spray as needed.
Better soil health	Use mulch, compost, rock powders, biostimulants.

PEACH TREE CURL

Controls	Application
Baking-soda spray	Spray in fall.
Garlic tea	Spray in fall.
Liquid copper products	Spray in fall.
Better soil health	Use mulch, compost, rock powders, and biostimulants.

SOOTY MOLD

Controls	Application
Baking-soda spray	Light spray as needed.
Beneficial insects	Ladybugs and green lacewings will control aphids whose honeydew causes the sooty mold.

WEEDS

Have you ever read anything good about the weeds? Unless you've read Malcolm Beck's *Lessons in Nature* or Charles Walters' *Weeds*, probably not!

Weeds are nature's greatest and most diverse group of plants. Even though many members of the weed fraternity are beautiful, man has been convinced by the herbicide fraternity to condemn the weeds and consider them his enemy. Mention weeds and most people think in terms of control through spraying chemicals. They rarely think of why the weeds grow or of their value.

Weeds are here on earth for very specific purposes. Different weeds have different jobs to do. Some are here to ensure that the soil always has the protection of a green blanket to shade and cool the ground. Others are here to prevent the erosion of bare soil. Others are here to help balance the minerals in the soil. Many weeds provide all these important functions.

Weeds take no chances. They germinate and spread to protect any soil left bare by man's mismanagement of the land. In every cubic foot of soil lie millions of weed seeds waiting to germinate when needed. When man strips the green growth off the land, weeds are needed. When hard winters freeze the ornamental lawn grasses, weeds are needed. When we mow too low and apply harsh chemicals to the soil, weeds are needed.

If it weren't for weeds, the topsoil of the earth would have eroded away years ago. Much of the topsoil has already gone from our farms forever to muddy our rivers and fill our lakes and eventually end up in the ocean.

It's a common misunderstanding that weeds rob our crops of moisture, sunlight, and nutrients. Weeds only borrow water and nutrients and eventually return it all to the soil for future crop use.

Weeds are tough. Rarely do you find weeds destroyed by insects or disease. Some weeds are pioneer plants as they are able to grow in soil unsuited for edible or domesticated plants. Weeds are able to build the soil with their strong and powerful roots that go deep, penetrating and loosening hard-packed soil. The deep roots bring minerals, especially trace elements, from the subsoil to the topsoil.

Weeds are indicators of certain soil deficiencies and actually collect or manufacture certain mineral elements that are lacking in the soil. This is nature's wonderful way of buffering and balancing the chemistry of soil.

Some weeds are good companion plants. Some have insect-repelling abilities, while others with deep roots help surface-feeding plants obtain moisture during dry spells. Weeds act as straws to bring water up from the deep, moist soil so that shallow-rooted plants can get some of the moisture.

Control becomes necessary when the vigorous weeds become too numerous in the fields and gardens. However, not understanding the dangers of spraying chemicals into the environment, many farmers, gardeners, and landscape people have primarily used powerful, toxic herbicides. Most herbicides upset or unbalance the harmony of the soil organisms, and some herbicides can persist in the soil for months. Even though microbes can repopulate after chemical treatment damage, they are slow to re-establish the complicated, natural balance.

There are safe and nonpolluting weed control methods such as mechanically aerating, mulching with organic materials, and using organic fertilizers to stimulate the growth of more desirable plants. The old, reliable methods of hand weeding, hoeing, and timely cultivating are not yet against the law and are good exercise.

The best weed control in turf is the following: Water deeply but infrequently, fertilize with 100% organic fertilizers, mow at a higher setting ($2^1/_2$-3"), and leave the clippings on the ground. Easy and effective weed control in the ornamental and vegetable beds is done by keeping a thick blanket of mulch on the bare soil at all times. Remember that clover, wild violets, and other herbs and wildflowers should sometimes be encouraged. Many plants that start out looking like noxious weeds end up presenting beautiful flower displays and wonderful fragrances.

Weed control starts with a new attitude about weeds. A few are acceptable, even beneficial.

ORGANIC WEED CONTROL

WEEDS (general)

Controls	Application
Vinegar	Spot spray 10% solution full strength on sunny day. 20% food grade is even better.
Chop with a hoe or hand remove	This is still legal!
Accept a few	Many "weeds" are herbs, wildflowers, and beneficial grasses.

BERMUDAGRASS, ST. AUGUSTINE

Controls	Application
Vinegar	Spray 20% food grade on hot, sunny day.
Dig out	Use a sod cutter or hoe to remove rhizomes and stolons.

NUTGRASS

Controls	Application
Aerify regularly	Use an extra amount of mechanical aerifying.
Mulch	Cover weeds in beds with a thick blanket of mulch.
Hand remove	

JOHNSONGRASS

Controls	Application
Physically remove	Can't stand to be mowed or regularly cut down.
NpHuric™	Spot spray @ 20% concentration.

CRABGRASS

Controls	Application
Fertilizer	Fertilize regularly with an organic fertilizer.
Mowing height	Mow at a height of 3" or more.

DALLISGRASS

Controls	Application
Vinegar	Spot spray with 20% food grade on a hot, sunny day.
NpHuric™	Spot spray @ 20% concentration.

POISON IVY

Controls	Application
Physically remove plants but protect skin	Do not attempt if you are highly allergic.
Tecnu™	Apply to skin to prevent or to relieve rash pain.

POND ALGAE*

Controls	Application
Tilapia fish	Release in spring after water temperature is above 60°
Water circulation	

POND WEEDS*

Organic Solution	Application
White Amur fish	Release in spring after water temperature is above 60°

*License for both these fish available through fish and wildlife departments.

MISCELLANEOUS ORGANIC CONTROL

STUPID NEIGHBORS

Control	Application
Try to help them	Give them the names of organic books to read; ask them to tune in to *The Natural Way* or WBAP from 8-12 on Sunday mornings and read "The Natural Way" in *The Dallas Morning News* on Fridays.

ALLERGIES

Control	Application
Mint and honey tea	10 cups of water, 5 sprigs spearmint, 2 applemint, 2 bee balm, 1 peppermint, 1 tablespoon honey, and a slice of lemon. Steep—don't boil, drink, and enjoy.

ORGANIC ANIMAL CONTROL

ARMADILLOS

Control	Application
Live traps	Pied Piper™ or Have a Heart™. Need to use batter boards to guide them into the trap.

BIRDS

Control	Application
Cats	I'd rather have the birds.
Soapy water	Last resort: spray roosting birds with a mild soap solution. Do in warm weather only.
Garlic/Pepper Spray	Most birds are beneficial and a natural mix of life in the garden will usually control populations.

CATS

Control	Application
Dogs	Or keep the cats indoors.
Citrus extract or peelings	Apply to problem areas.
Live traps	Pied Piper™ or Have a Heart™.
Dry cayenne or other hot pepper	Spread around problem area.

DEER

Control	Application
Hinder™	Apply per label.
Soap bar	Hang in trees in problem areas.
Blood meal	Spread around problem area.

DOGS

Control	Application
Live traps	Pied Piper™ or Have a Heart™.
Dog runs	It is not cruel to house dogs in dog runs when not at home.
Dog-B-Gone™ home brew	1 part cayenne pepper, 2 parts mustard powder, 2 parts flour, or use straight cayenne or other hot pepper.

GOPHERS

Control	Application
Black Hole Gopher Trap™	Install in tunnel per instructions.
Gopher spurge	Plant gopher spurge, Euphobia lathyrus around the perimeter of problem area.
Garlic	Plant as a barrier to garden areas.
Other metal traps	Install in tunnels per instructions.

MICE

Control	Application
Traps	Still looking for a better one.
Baits	Apply Assault™ in bait station.
Cats	The natural way.
Peppermint	Use ground-up pieces of mint or cardboard soaked in peppermint oil as repellent.

MOLES

Control	Application
Same as for gophers	At least you have nice, sandy soil.

RABBITS

Control	Application
Low and recessed fences	Electric fences are even better.
Cayenne or other pepper	Dust onto problem area.
Blood meal	Spread around problem area.

RACCOONS

Control	Application
Live traps	Pied Piper™ or Have a Heart™.

RATS

Control	Application
Death traps	Still looking for a better one.
Live traps	Pied Piper™ or Have a Heart™.
Bait stations	Assault™ per label.

SKUNKS

Control	Application
Live traps	Pied Piper™ or Have a Heart™.
	Be careful of the spray and bites. Many skunks are rabid.

SNAKES

Control	Application
Introduce bull and king snakes	These guys look fierce but are great friends.
Roadrunners, guineas, and other snake-eating birds	They control the dangerous snakes like rattlers, copperheads, coral, and water moccasins.
Most garden snakes are beneficial	Protect nature's biodiversity.

SQUIRRELS

Control	Application
Live traps	Pied Piper™ or Have a Heart™.
Fox urine	Apply liquid to problem areas. Works as a repellent.
Blood meal and/or cayenne or other hot pepper	Spread around problem area.

TURTLES

Control	Application
Underwater traps for aquatic turtles	Pied Piper™.
Land turtles are mostly beneficial	Fence off vegetable garden.

7

PRODUCTS

PRODUCTS

ORGANIC FERTILIZERS

Organic fertilizers nourish and improve the soil. As opposed to synthetic fertilizers, they help the soil because they do not create high levels of salts and nitrates in the soil, which kill or repel beneficial soil organisms. By composition, organic fertilizers release nutrients slowly and naturally. All components in an organic fertilizer are usable by the plants, since there are no useless fillers such as exist in synthetic fertilizers.

The nitrogen-phosphorus-potassium analysis (N-P-K) printed on bags of fertilizer by law is basically irrelevant in an organic program. Feeding the soil and plants with nothing but nitrogen, phosphorous, and potassium is like feeding your kids nothing but cheese. Soil and people need a balance of nutrients. For some unknown reason, fertilizer recommendations continue to emphasize these three nutrients with special emphasis on high levels of nitrogen. A standard obsolete recommendation is a ra-

tio of 3-1-2 or 4-1-2, such as 15-5-10 or 16-4-8.

Studies at the Department of Agronomy at Alabama Polytechnic University show that as much as 50% of all synthetic nitrogen applied to the soil will be leached out, and the half that does reach the plant may be harmful. Other studies show that an excess of chemical fertilizer slows or even stops the activity of microflora and microfauna such as beneficial bacteria, algae, fungi, and other microorganisms. Harsh fertilizers also cause damage to macroorganisms, such as earthworms, millipedes, centipedes, etc., which are extremely important to the natural processes in the soil.

High-nitrogen fertilizers also can cause severe thatch buildup in lawns by forcing unnatural flushes of green growth. That's why mechanical thatch removal programs are often recommended for chemically maintained lawns. Organic lawn care programs take care of thatch problems naturally as the living microorganisms feed on the grass clippings and other dead organic matter.

High-nitrogen fertilizers such as 15-5-10 (or even higher) are still being recommended by many in the landscaping business. I've made the same recommendations myself in the past, but those amounts of nitrogen, phosphorous, and potassium are unnecessary and even damaging to soil health.

When healthy, the soil will produce and release nutrients during the decomposition process. The microbiotic activity releases tied up trace elements such as iron, zinc, boron, chlorine, copper, magnesium, molybdenum, and others, which are all important to a well-balanced soil.

One of the most important fertilizers in an organic program is organic matter, which becomes humus during the decomposition process. Humus becomes humic acid—one of the active ingredients of organic matter.

Organic fertilizers are better than artificial products because they are the derivatives of plants and therefore contain all the trace elements that exist in growing plants, probably all 92 basic elements. Synthetic fertilizers do not have this rounded balance of mineral nutrients.

In addition, organic fertilizers are naturally slow release and provide nutrients to plants when they need the nutrients. Synthetic fertilizers glut the plants with nutrients immediately after application, which is usually at the wrong time.

My definition of a fertilizer is anything that increases soil health to stimulate plant growth.

ORGANIC FERTILIZERS

AGRI GRO: A liquid biostimulant that contains enzymes and living microorganisms used with an organic fertility program. Agri Gro™ provides impressive growth and production-quality increases. Works best when mixed with molasses.

AGRISPON: A liquid, metabolic stimulator that encourages root growth and top growth and helps control pathogens of all sorts indirectly through biological activity. It's used for soil, foliage, and seed treatment to enhance plant growth and health. It reduces drought stress and salt stress and makes better use of all fertilizer elements, especially nitrogen. By increasing microbial activity, Agrispon increases nitrogen fixation by microorganisms.

ALFALFA MEAL: Alfalfa provides many nutritional benefits not only for plant use, but for soil organisms as well. One very important ingredient is triacontanol, a powerful plant growth regulator. Orchid and rose growers make an alfalfa tea and spray it directly on as a foliar fertilizer. Alfalfa is very high in vitamins, plus N-P-K, Ca, Mg, and other valuable minerals. It also includes sugars, starches, proteins, fiber, and 16 amino acids. Sprinkle lightly over garden and water, or use about a handful (depending on the size) around each rose, tree, or shrub.

Alfalfa Tea: In a 5-gallon bucket, put 1 cup alfalfa meal. Fill bucket with water; let it set overnight. The result will be a thick tea. Apply generously to the root area of shrubs and flowers or use as a foliar spray after straining.

BAT GUANO: A natural, all-purpose fertilizer containing nitrogen and lots of trace elements. The analysis will vary with the age of the guano. It has natural fungicidal qualities and has almost no chance of being contaminated with pesticides or chemicals. It is an excellent supplemental fertilizer for flowers. Best to apply once or twice during the growing season. It looks mild but has as much as 10% nitrogen, so be careful not to overuse.

BIOFORM: Excellent Liquid fertilizer made from fish emulsion, seaweed, and molasses. The analysis is 4-2-4-3S. The sulfur in the molasses has virtually eliminated the fish smell. The product contains a biostimulant/soil penetrant.

BIOSTIMULATORS: Also called biostimulants, these materials are usually liquid and contain various minerals, enzymes, vitamins, and sometimes microbes to stimulate or activate the biological activity on plants and in the soil. Products in this catagory include Agrispon™, Agri Gro™, Nitron A-35™, Molasses, sugar, Pent-A-Vate™, vinegar, and H_2O_2.

BLOOD MEAL: Excellent organic source of nitrogen and phosphorous. Good to use as a mix with cottonseed meal. Expensive but good to use occasionally. Analysis can range from 12-2-1 to 11-0-0.

BONE MEAL: Good source of calcium and phosphorous recommended for bulbs, tomatoes, and other vegetables. Analysis will range from 2-12-0 to 4-12-0 with 2%-5% calcium.

CATTLE MANURE: Manure is one of our greatest natural resources. It has to be handled properly and not overused in any one area. Using too much of anything can cause problems. Manure can be properly used in several ways. Cow manure is a good ingredient for the manufacture of compost or for use directly on agricultural fields. Dairy cow manure is best because it has the least chance of chemical contamination. It should be composted prior to using in the home vegetable garden. Hog manure has similar properties and uses, but it has a higher analysis, usually around 2-5-1 compared to cattle manure's 2-1-1.

CEDAR FLAKES: Good for chiggers, fleas, and lowering the pH of the soil. An excellent material to use on the floor of greenhouses. Cedar flakes are an excellent control for harmful nematodes. Would be a staple organic product if a certain institution hadn't sabotoged it.

CHELATORS: Chelated iron and other chelated nutrients are used when a direct dose of a particular nutrient is needed to quickly solve a deficiency. Chelated products are organic compounds with attached inorganic metal molecules, which are more available for plant use. Compost, humus, humic acid, and microorganisms have natural chelating properties.

CHICKEN LITTER: Chicken litter is a good natural fertilizer high in nitrogen. Pelletized forms are better because they are not as dusty. Approximate analysis is 6-4-2. Unfortunately, commercial chickens are still being fed lots of unnatural things. Best to compost before using.

COLLOIDAL PHOSPHATE: A mixture of fine particles of phosphate suspended in a clay base. Economic form of natural phosphorous and calcium. Unlike chemically made phosphates, rock phosphate is insoluble in water, will not leach away, and therefore is long-lasting. Has 18% phosphorous and 15% calcium as well as trace elements. Florida is the primary source.

COMPOST: The best fertilizer and the key to any organic program. Nature's own product, high in nutrient humus, humic acid, and microorganisms. Compost has magical healing and growing powers and can be used successfully on any and all plants. Analysis will vary due to ingredients. Compost can be made at home or purchased commercially. The best composts are those made from a variety of organic materials such as hay, sawdust, paunch manure, leaves, twigs, bark, wood chips, dead plants, nongreasy food scraps, pecan hulls, grass clippings, and animal manure. The manure percentage in compost should not be more than 20-25% of the volume. The best manure to use is whatever is locally available: chicken, turkey, cattle, horse, rabbit, etc.

COTTONSEED MEAL: A good natural fertilizer with an acid pH. Analysis will vary and ranges from 6-2-1 to 7-2-2 with trace elements. Does have odor. Good organic source of nitrogen.

EARTH-RITE PRODUCTS: A line of humus-based products that also provide N-P-K and trace elements.

EARTH SAFE: A line of organic fertilizers owned by the Carl Pool Company. Turf Toughener™ is an all-natural turf fertilizer made from molasses, feather meal, meat and bone meal, blood meal, alfalfa meal, fish meal, and cottonseed and soybean meals. Analysis is 4-1-5, tomato and vegetable food is 4-6-5, premium lawn food is 9-3-6.

EARTHWORM CASTINGS: An effective organic fertilizer that is high in bacteria, calcium, iron, magnesium, and sulphur as well as N-P-K and has over 60 trace minerals. Earthworm castings make an excellent ingredient in potting soil, in flats when germinating seed, and to toss into each hole when planting vegetables, herbs, or ornamentals.

FERTILAID: Outstanding all-purpose fertilizer made of tankage (blood meal, bone meal, and natural urea), chicken and fish waste, 37 cultures of soil-borne bacteria, 28 trace elements, 20% humus, 20% humic acid. It is a good soil detoxifier and many users say that it has fungicidal properties. Its only drawbacks are dustiness and consistency. Great product but unfortunately off the market as of this printing.

FISH EMULSION: A concentrated liquid fish fertilizer for use directly in the soil or as a foliar feed. The analysis will range from 4-1-1 to 5-2-2. It is reported to be a very effective insecticide. Great all-purpose spray when mixed with liquid kelp. Has an odor for about 24 hours—a pretty strong one, in fact.

FISH MEAL: A natural fertilizer originally used in this country by Native Americans growing corn. Has a high analysis of approximately 8-12-2 but is also stinky, so use with caution.

GLAUCONITE: (See greensand)

GRANITE SAND: Sand-like residue from the granite quarry or natural deposits. Excellent way to add minerals to planting beds. Much better than sharp sand. Contains 5% potash and many trace minerals.

GREENSAND: A material called glauconite, which is a naturally deposited undersea, iron-potassium silicate. It's an excellent source of potash with a normal analysis of 0-1-5. It's best used with other fertilizers.

GREENSENSE: A granulated, organic fertilizer made from composted animal manure, activated charcoal, alfalfa, molasses, and iron sulfate which offers a quick greening effect. Pelletizing eliminated the dust problem, and the molasses took care of the manure odor.

GRO-UP: Organic fertilizer containing cricket castings, ground crawfish, crab shells, rock phosphate and feather meal.

GYPSUM: This natural material is calcium sulfate and is an excellent source of calcium and sulfur. Gypsum also neutralizes plant toxins, removes salts from the soil, and opens the soil structure to promote aeration and drainage. Gypsum is approximately 23% calcium and 17% sulfate.

HORSE MANURE: Horse manure is higher in nitrogen than most other farm animal manures and is an excellent material to use for the manufacture of compost. Fresh manures should not be tilled directly into the soil unless they are applied a month before planting or composted first. Sheep manure has similar properties and uses.

HUMATES: Leonardite shale is basically low-grade lignite coal and is a good carbon source. Percentage of humic acid will vary. May be made into liquid form or used in the dry form. Excellent source of humic acid and trace minerals.

HYDROGEN PEROXIDE: A natural oxidizing material. For use on soil in diluted amounts. A dangerous product in concentrated forms.

KELP MEAL: A dry fertilizer made from seaweed. Approximate analysis 1-0-8, lots of trace minerals, and an excellent source of plant hormones, which stimulate root growth and regulate plant growth. Seaweed also provides soil-conditioning substances,improve the crumb structure or tilth.

KRICKET KRAP: 100% all-natural cricket manure from Augusta, Georgia. The fish-bait crickets are fed a high-protein diet of fish meal, soybean, blood meal, chicken chowder, corn, and molasses. Analysis is 4.63-3.07-2.00 plus magnesium and calcium. Rate is 10 lbs. per 1,000 sq. ft. spring and fall.

LAVA DUST: The sand-sized and smaller waste material left from lava gravel is an excellent, high-energy soil-amendment material. It can be used in potting soils and bed preparation.

LEATHER TANKAGE:
Leather tankage is a slaughter house by-product high in nitrogen. It will not burn or leach. Several organic fertilizers are derived from leather tankage. Some tankage contains chemicals used in the tanning process.

LIME: A major calcium fertilizer, dolomitic lime contains 30-35% magnesium. High-cal lime contains only 10% magnesium. High-cal is preferred because most low calcium soils usually contain too much magnesium.

MAESTRO-GRO: A line of organic fertilizers that have a bone meal base. Products include a wide variety of ingredients such as bone meal, fish meal, feather meal, rock phosphates, kelp meal, greensand, and microorganisms.

MANALFA: Cross between alfalfa and cow manure. Be careful using products pelletized with clay which might cause a buildup over time.

MEDINA: A dairy cow manure extract used for stimulation of microorganisms in the soil. Medina Plus™ contains trace elements and seaweed as an added benefit. Hastagro™, a Medina product, is a low-chemical fertilizer with an analysis of 6-12-6. It also contains seaweed.

MILORGANITE: Sewer-sludge fertilizer from Milwaukee. Has been widely used on golf courses. Had a scare for a while that the product caused Lou Gehrig's disease but this was proven to be false. It's best not to use any sewer sludge product on edible plants.

MOLASSES: Sweet syrup used as a soil amendment to feed and stimulate microorganisms. Contains sulfur, potash, and other trace minerals.

NATURE SAFE: Organic fertilizer composed primarily of slaughter house by-products.

ORGANIGRO: Organic fertilizer containing poultry litter, blood meal, feather meal, Sul-Po-Mag, kelp meal and bat guano.

PENT-A-VATE: Liquid biostimulant used to accelerate microbiotic activity and loosen soil. It is one of the ingredients in Bioform™.

RABBIT MANURE: The average analysis of rabbit manure is around 2.5-1.5-5. Mixed with leaves, sawdust, straw, grass, and other vegetative materials, it makes an excellent compost. Can be used directly as a fertilizer, but it's better to compost first.

RINGER: Ringer is the brand name of a group of natural products for landscaping, lawns, and vegetable gardens. The base for the products is chicken feathers, blood meal, soybean meal, and bone meal. The products contain soil microorganisms and enzymes as well as organic matter.

ROOT STIMULATORS: This is a generic term that refers to mild fertilizers or any material that stimulates microbial activity and root growth: seaweed, Agrispon™, Medina™, Agri Gro™, Nitron A-35™, Carl Pool Root Stimulator™, SuperThrive™.

SEAWEED: Best used as a foliar spray. Excellent source of trace minerals. Should be used often. Contains hormones that stimulate root growth and branching. The 55 trace elements found in seaweed are present in the proportions they are found in plants.

SEAWEED, LIQUID (Kelp): A product made from seaweed that will green plants quickly. Loaded with trace elements and hormones, and acts as a root stimulator. Makes excellent all-purpose spray mixed with fish emulsion, which fertilizes and helps control insects and fungi. Also acts as a chelating agent, making other fertilizers and nutrients more available to the plants.

SEWER SLUDGE: Most cities produce this product. It is an excellent lawn fertilizer but probably should not be used on vegetables or other edible plants.

SOIL-SUL: A Carl Pool product that is mixed at 2 cups per 5 gal.— to cure chlorosis and root rot.

SUL-PO-MAG: A mined source of sulfur, potassium, and magnesium. A naturally occurring mineral containing 22% sulfur, 22% potash, and 11.1% magnesium. It is naturally granulated.

SULFUR: A basic mineral often lacking in alkaline soils. Applying granulated sulfur at 5 to 10 lbs./1,000 sq. ft. twice annually can bring base saturation of calcium down and raise magnesium. Be careful not to breath dust, overapply, or use when planting seed. It can act as a preemergent. Sulfur dust is also used as a pesticide in some situations.

SUPERTHRIVE: A liquid product made from vitamins and hormones. Excellent supplemental food for flowering plants. Use at 3 drops per gallon at each watering for best results. Can be mixed with other products.

SUSTANE: A manufactured fertilizer made from composted turkey manure.

FERTILIZER CHART

Organic Fertilizers	N	P	K	Comments
Alfalfa	3	1	2	Vitamin A, folic acid, trace minerals, and growth hormone "tricontanol."
Bat guano	10	3	1	High in nitrogen, phosphorous, and trace minerals.
Blood meal	12	1	1	Good nitrogen source but smelly.
Bone meal	2	12	0	Good calcium and phosphorous source.
Cow manure	2	1	1	Best to use in composted form to avoid weed seed.
Colloidal phosphate	0	18	0	Excellent organic source of phosphorous, calcium, and trace minerals.
Compost	1	1	1	Best all-around organic fertilizer.
Cottonseed meal	7	2	2	Acid pH, lots of trace minerals.
Earthworm castings	1	.1	.1	Beneficial bacteria, trace minerals, humus, earthworm eggs.
Fish emulsion	5	2	2	Foliar plant food, helps with insect control, stinks!
Fish meal	7	13	3	Nitrogen, phosphorous, and lots of vitamins and minerals but smelly.
Granite sand	0	0	5	Low cost Source of minerals, especially potash.
Greensand	0	2	5	Natural source of phosphorous, potash, and trace minerals.
Horse manure	4	1	1	More powerful than cow manure.
Molasses	1	0	5	Food for microorganisms and source of sulfur and potash.
Rabbit manure	3	2	1	Not used enough, excellent source of natural nutrition.
Pig manure	.5	.3	.5	Good source of humus and microorganisms.
Poultry manure	5	3	2	High-nitrogen organic fertilizer, best to compost first.
Sheep manure	.5	.3	5	Good natural fertilizer.
Seaweed (dry)	1	0	1	Trace minerals and hormones that stimulate root growth and branching.
Seaweed (liquid)	1	0	1	Same as dry but can be used as a foliar spray.
Sludge compost	5	3	0	OK in the lawn but don't use on the veggie garden.
Sul-Po-Mag	0	0	22	Mined source of sulfur, potassium, and magnesium.
Tankage	6	8	0	Slaughter house by-product.

MANUFACTURED FERTILIZERS

Organic Fertilizers	N	P	K	Comments
Agrispon	0	0	0	Growth stimulator, increases all plant and soil processes.
Bioform	4	2	4	Fish emulsion, seaweed, and molasses.
GreenSense	3	1	2	Composted manure, activated carbon, alfalfa, molasses, ferrous sulfate.
Fertilaid	4	2	0	Slaughterhouse waste, urea, and microorganisms.
Maestro-Gro	6	2	4	Fish meal, bone meal, and other natural ingredients.
Tomas	8	2	8	Feather meal, bone meal,and other natural ingredients.
Ringer	9	4	4	Feather meal, fish meal, & other natural ingredients.
Sustane	5	2	4	Composted turkey manure.

Granulated and has some odor for 24-36 hours. Has shown excellent soil improvement and reduction of diseases.

TOMAS: A manufactured organic fertilizer containing a variety of ingredients such as feather meal, fish meal, and bone. Analysis will vary due to different formulations. Has an interesting marketing plan.

TURKEY MANURE: Turkey manure is a high-nitrogen manure that is an excellent ingredient for compost making.

ZINC: Important fertilizer element for pecans and other crops. Will defoliate fruit trees if misused. Not needed in acid soils or balanced soils. Zinc is a trace element found in most organic fertilizers. The definition of a good organic product is this, "any material that when applied improves the balance and health of the soil."

FOLIAR FEEDING

Feeding the soil is the basis of organics. I know I say that a lot, but since nothing else is really very important, what else can I do? However, there are ways of stimulating the natural processes in the soil and in the plants without putting the material into the soil. Spraying the foliage of plants can provide some significant horticultural advantages.

Some foliar sprays such as fish emulsion and seaweed are fertilizers. When fertilizer nutrients are sprayed directly on the foliage, immediate results can often be seen because the micronutrients, when taken in through the foliage, are immediately available to the plant.

When food crops or ornamentals have a chlorotic symptom (yellow leaves with green veins) resulting from lack of iron or other soil elements, spraying the foliage with a chelated product can create a greening improvement within a few days. Plants need green foliage to be able to produce food through the process of photosynthesis where sunlight, water, and carbon dioxide combine in the leaves to produce sugars and carbohydrates to feed the plant.

Some spray products are stimulators rather than feeders. Agrispon™, Medina™, and other biological products stimulate plant growth and flower/fruit production by increasing photosynthesis in the foliage, increasing the movement of fluids and energy within the plant, increasing root exudates and microbiotic activity in the soil at the root zone, and increasing the uptake of nutrients from the soil through the root hairs. In other words, foliar feeding can provide missing or "locked up" elements as well as stimulate all of the natural systems in the plant and in the soil. The end result is bigger, stronger, healthier plants with increased drought, insect, and disease resistance.

Here are some points to remember when using foliar sprays:

1 Less is usually better in foliar sprays. Light, regularly applied sprays are better than heavy, infrequent blasts. Mists of liquids are better than big drops.

2 High humidity increases a leaf's ability to absorb liquids. Spraying on damp mornings or evenings will increase the effectiveness of the spray. The small openings (stomata) on the leaves close up during the heat of the day so that moisture within the plant is preserved. The best time of day to spray is late afternoon.

3 Young foliage seems to absorb nutrients better than old, hard foliage. Therefore, foliar feeding is most effective during the periods of new growth on plants.

4 Adding sugar or molasses in small amounts to your spray solutions can stimulate the growth of beneficial microorganisms on the leaf surfaces. The stimulation of friendly microbes helps to fight off the harmful pathogens. For the skeptics who regularly read my stuff trying to find points that are unprovable—don't try to understand this specific point, just accept it—it works.

5 Foliar feeding will increase the storage life of food crops. It will also increase cold and heat tolerance.

Organic foliar feedings can help control insects and disease as well as fertilize and stimulate plants. The simple mixture of fish emulsion and seaweed makes an excellent all-purpose foliar spray for an organic program. It has been used for years by organic gardeners and is still hard to beat. The mix most used is 1 tablespoon of seaweed and 4 tablespoons of fish emulsion per gallon of water. Nonphosphate soaps are sometimes used as wetting agents, but remember that surfactants in general are very harmful to microorganisms.

Foliar feeding has been used since 1844 when it was discovered that plant nutrients could be leached from leaves by rain. Experiments soon proved that nutrients could also enter the plant through the foliage. It's still somewhat of a mystery as to just exactly how the nutrients enter the plant through the foliage—but it is known and agreed that

*Foliar feeding is an excellent way to give plants
fertilizer elements that are lacking in the soil.*

it works and works quickly. For something further to think about, there is also evidence that nutrients can be absorbed through the bark of trees. Spray away!

ORGANIC PEST CONTROL PRODUCTS

The following products and techniques are a guide for controlling insects with the least damage to nature's balances. The organic pesticides are better than the chemical pesticides, but I hope you can learn to use any of them only as a last resort since most of the pesticides can't tell the difference between a good bug and a bad one.

ANTIDESICCANTS: Also called antitranspirants, these products are made from pine oil and are nontoxic and biodegradable. They are sometimes used for the prevention of powdery mildew on roses and crape myrtles. They work by spreading a clear film over the leaves.

BACILLUS THURINGIENSIS (Bt): A beneficial bacteria applied as a spray to kill caterpillars. Sold under a variety of names such as Thuricide™, Dipel™, and Bio-Worm. Use *Bacillus thuringiensis* "Israelensis" (Bti) in water for mosquitos. Use Bioform™ with Bt for extra effect. Sugar in the molasses provides protein and keeps insect-killing bacteria alive on the foliage longer—even during rain. Bt "San Diego" is good for Colorado potato beetle, elm leaf beetle, and other leaf-chewing beetles.

BAKING SODA: Mixed at the rate of 4 teaspoons per gallon, baking soda makes an excellent fungicide for black spot, powdery mildew, brown patch, and other fungal problems. Be careful to keep the spray on the foliage and not on the soil as much as possible. Baking soda is composed of sodium and bicarbonate—both are necessary in the soil but only in very small amounts.

BIODEGRADABLE SOAP: Nonphosphate liquid soaps and water mixed together into a spray make a good control for aphids and other small insects. Safer™, Greenlight™, and Ortho™ make excellent insecticidal soaps, and environmental-type soaps such as Neo-Life Green™, Natural Green™, and Shaklee's Basic-H™ make an effective spray when mixed in a mild solution with water. Strong solutions can damage plant foliage, and even weak solutions can kill many of the microscopic beneficial insects and microorganisms—so use sparingly.

BLACK HOLE GOPHER TRAP: Guaranteed to trap your gophers, so the ad says. Gophers are notoriously hard to get rid of—and annoyingly destructive.

Even if they don't wolf down your entire harvest-to-be, their tunnels and mounds can ruin your garden. The black hole trap works only on gophers and is safe around pets and children. Gophers live in round tunnels and have learned that square things (like most traps) are dangerous, so this trap is round, like the tunnels. When the trap is placed at the end of its tunnel, the gopher detects the air and light that the trap lets in. When it rushes to plug it up, a snare catches and kills it.

BORDEAUX MIX: A fungicide and insecticide usually made from copper sulfate and lime. Good for most foliar problems and an effective organic treatment for disease control on fruits, vegetables, shrubs, trees, and flowers such as anthracnose, botrytis blight, peach tree curl, and twig blight. Wet down decks and other hard surfaces before spraying. Some staining is possible.

COPPER: Trace mineral that in liquid form is an effective fungicide for powdery mildew, black spot, peach leaf curl, and other diseases. Copper is also an ingredient in Bordeaux mix.

DEMIZE: Demize™ is a citrus-oil extract used for killing fleas indoors. It is not a true organic product but has low toxicity, has a fresh, citrus fragrance, and works quite well. This and other products such as Flea Stop are d-Limonene.

DIACIDE (Now called Perma-Guard): A product containing diatomaceous earth and pyrethrum, a natural insecticide derived from a species of chrysanthemum (*C. coccineum*). Will kill aphids, beetles, leafhoppers, worms, caterpillars, and ants on contact. Relatively nontoxic to animals and people. Apply at the first sign of an insect problem but do not use as a preventative.

DIATOMACEOUS EARTH (D. E.): Diatomaceous earth is approximately 23% calcium, 12% silicon, and 57% carbonate. It is skeletal remains of microscopic organisms (1-celled aquatic plants) that lived in seawater millions of years ago in the western United States. The broken skeletons have razor sharp edges that scratch the exoskeletons of insects, causing them to desiccate and die. Apply using a dusting machine (manual or electrostatic) covering plants or lawn areas entirely. Be sure to use a dust mask when applying! A better way to apply is to mix 2 tablespoons of diatomaceous earth in 1 gallon of water and spray as a liquid. D.E. is nonselective, so use sparingly. Breathing dusty material can cause lung problems. As a food supplement for pets or livestock—use as 1-2% of the food volume.

DORMANT OIL: Long-standing, organic, winter treatment for scale and other over-wintering insects. Petroleum-based and will kill beneficial insects, so use sparingly. It's recommended to spray dormant oil at temperatures between 40° and 80°. It works by smothering the over-wintering insects. Effective against scale, aphids, spider mites, and others. Do not use sulfur as a fungicide without waiting 30 days after using dormant oil.

FLOATING GRO-COVER: Gardening fabric designed to envelope plants in a moist, greenhouse warmth while allowing water, light, and ventilation for proper plant respiration. Protects foliage from chewing insects, prevents flies and moths from laying maggot or caterpillar eggs, and reduces diseases carried by pests. Birds, rabbits, and other animals are discouraged from feeding on plants. On the other hand, it looks bad and gets in the way.

GARLIC/PEPPER TEA: An organic insect- and disease-control material made from the juice of garlic and hot peppers such as jalapeño, habeñero, or cayenne. This is one of the few preventative controls that I recommend. It is effective for both ornamental and food crops.

GENCOR: Growth regulator for roaches. Not a true organic but a low-toxicity choice for problem infestations.

IMIDAN: Imidan is reported to be the best control for plum curculio, which damages apples, plums, peaches, and other stone fruits. Imidan is a chemical pesticide but seems to be the least-toxic choice. Apply at petal fall and 10 days later.

LIME SULFUR: An organic fungicide (calcium polysulfide) for fruits, berries, roses, nuts, and ornamental plants. Spray plants as buds swell, but before they open. It is effective for powdery mildew, anthracnose, peach leaf curl, brown rot. Insects it controls include scale and mites.

LIQUID COPPER: A flowable formulation of copper salts for fungal control on roses, vegetables, fruits, and ornamentals. It is a good control of powdery mildew, bacterial blights, and anthracnose.

NICOTINE SULFATE: An oldtime, organic pesticide used for the control of hard-to-kill insects. Although it is a quickly biodegradable product, it is dangerous to handle and should only be used as a last resort. Remember how dangerous nicotine is the next time you light up. It is one of the few effective controls for cutter ants.

NOSEMA LOCUSTAE: A biological control for crickets and grasshoppers. It works the same way Bt works on caterpillars. It's applied as a dry bait and the insects eat the material, get sick, and are cannibalized by their friends. Charming, isn't it? But it works. Brand names include Nolo Bait™, Grasshopper Attack™, and Semispore™.

OILS: There are now four types of spray oils: dormant, summer, horticultural, and vegetable. Dormant oils are petroleum based, relatively free of impurities, and have been used as far back as 1880. Dormant oils have lower volatility and more insect-killing power than the other oils, but they can be more toxic to plants. These oils should only be used during the winter months when plants are dormant. Summer oils, also petroleum based, are lighter, less poisonous to plants, more volatile, and less effective on insects. They can be used during the heat of summer on some hard-to-kill bugs. Horticultural oils are the lightest and most pure petroleum oils. They can be used for spraying pecan trees and fruit trees, but they are also effective on shrubs and flowers that have scale or other insect infestations. Vegetable oils are plant extracts. They are environmentally safe, degrade quickly by evaporation, fit into organic or integrated pest management programs, are nonpoisonous to the applicator, are noncorrosive to the spray equipment, and kill a wide range of insects. The state of Texas is leaning toward vegetable oils. Drilling lubricants can no longer be petroleum oils.

PRECOR: An insect growth regulator that controls fleas by preventing the larvae from developing into adults. It is often used indoors with Demize™. It's not a true organic but fits into an organic program because of its low toxicity. Also sold as Ovitrol™ and Fleatrol™. They are all methoprene, PBO, and pyrethrins.

PYRETHRUM: Available in liquid or dry forms. Will kill a wide range of insects including aphids, beetles, leafhoppers, worms, caterpillars, and ants. It is short-lived and relatively nontoxic to animals. Pyrethrum is ground painted daisy (*chrysanthemum coccineum*). Artificial substitutes, called pyrethroids, should be avoided. Pyrethrin is the active ingredient in the natural product.

ROTENONE: 1% solution can be used to kill aphids, worms, beetles, borers, and thrips. 5% solution is effective for use on fire ants and hard-to-kill type beetles. Dangerous if not handled carefully, but still considered an acceptable organic product. Products available containing rotenone and pyrethrum.

RYANIA: Root extract from the ryania shrub. Can be used as dust or spray to control moths, corn borer, and other problem insects. Ryania is a relatively strong organic pesticide.

SABADILLA: Made from a tropical lily. Effective on some of the hard-to-kill garden pests such as thrips, cabbage worms, grasshoppers, loopers, leafhoppers, harlequin bugs, adult squash beetles, and cucumber beetles. Relatively nontoxic to man.

SULFUR: Finely ground sulfur is used by mixing with water or dusting on dry plants to control black spot, leaf spot, brown canker, rust, peach leaf curl, powdery mildew, apple scab, and many insect pests. Mix with liquid seaweed to enhance fungicidal properties. Sulfur will also control fleas, mites, thrips, and chiggers. To avoid leaf burn, do not use when temperature is 90° or above.

TANGLEFOOT: Spread on the bark of trees to control gypsy moths, canker worms, climbing cutworms, and ants. Made from natural gum resins, castor oil, and vegetable waxes. Old product that's useful in all organic programs.

TRIPLE ACTION 20: Triple Action 20™ is a synthetic fungicide but has extremely low toxicity and biodegrades very quickly. It gives excellent control of fireblight. Use at 1 teaspoon per gallon. Also sold as Consan 20™.

VINEGAR: Vinegar can be an effective tool for controlling a few problem fire-ant mounds. Pour it directly into the center of the mound. Use the strongest dilution available. 5% and 10% vinegar are commonly available in the grocery store. Vinegar is an effective herbicide on a hot, sunny day, especially 20% food grade. It's a nonselective herbicide, so be careful to keep it off your good plants.

WEED FABRIC: Synthetic fabric that allows air and water movement, while at the same time blocking out some weed growth. For use in all gardening areas and under walkways, driveways, decks, and patios. Not recommended. Use mulch in order to maintain the natural processes in the soil.

YELLOW STICKY TRAPS: Nontoxic, bright-yellow cards that trap insects with their sticky coating. They are also used to monitor insect populations. Particularly effective in greenhouses.

COMPOST—MOTHER NATURE'S FERTILIZER

What is compost? How do you make compost? Is compost a fertilizer? How do I use compost? Is composted manure in a bag really compost? Do I need bark, peat moss, and compost?

To answer all these questions, let's go through the entire composting process. For starters, everything on earth that's alive dies and everything that dies rots, and completely rotted material is compost. Yes, compost is a fertilizer. In fact, it is the best fertilizer—being nature's own. Compost is not only an excellent fertilizer but also an excellent way to recycle waste. The word compost comes from two Latin words meaning "bring together."

The best composts are those that are made at home from several ingredients. The ideal mixture is 80% vegetative matter and 20% animal waste. The best materials are those that you have on your own property. The second-best materials are those that can be easily gotten from near your property. The compost pile location can be in sun or shade, and covers are not necessary.

Even though there are many recipes for compost, it's almost impossible to foul up the compost-making process. For new gardens or planting beds, the composting can be done right on the ground by lightly tilling organic matter into the soil and mulching. To use this method effectively, it's best to do the work now and wait until next season to plant. Composting in the ground, as the forest does, simply takes longer than composting in a pile. Remember that composting is more of an art than a science and a little experimenting is good. There are many acceptable ways to build compost piles, but I find that the simplest systems are usually the best.

The best time to compost is whenever the raw materials are available. It's ideal to have compost piles working year round. Choose a convenient site—some easily accessible, utility area such as behind the garage or in the dog run. The most effective compost piles are made on a paved surface so that the liquid leachate can be caught and used as a fertilizer. When the pile is on the ground, the leachate is wasted but the earthworms can enter the pile and help complete the natural degradation of the material.

Next, decide what kind of a container to use. I don't use a container at all but instead just pile the material on the ground or on a concrete slab. If you choose to use a container, buy some hog wire, lumber, wooden pallets, cinder blocks, or any materials that will hold a volume of about 4'x4' with a height of 3 feet. I would say a minimum compost pile should be 3'x3'x3'.

Hay or wheat-straw bales make an excellent container for compost. Build a 2- or 3-sided container by stacking the bales to make the sides. At the end of the composting process, the hay-bale sides can be pulled into the mix to become part of the compost.

Many materials can be used to make compost. Some include grass clippings, leaves of all kinds, sawdust, spent plants, weeds (don't worry about the weed seed), tree chips, coffee grounds, feather meal, seaweed, peanut hulls, pecan hulls and other nut shells, fish scraps, brewery waste, slaughterhouse waste, pine needles, wool, silk, cotton, granite dust, uncooked vegetable scraps, fruit peelings and waste, pet hair, household dust, and animal manures. It's controversial whether dog and cat manure should be used in the compost pile. I don't have cats but I do use the dog manure. You should make your own decision on this point. I do not recommend using greasy or cooked foods, newspaper or other dyed or printed materials, synthetic fabrics, burned charcoal, plastics, rubber.

The materials should be chopped into various-size pieces and thoroughly mixed together. Compost piles that contain nothing but one particle size will not breathe properly. Layering the ingredients, as most books recommend, is unnecessary unless it will help to get the proportions right. Remember that after the first turning the layers won't be there anymore. Also remember that green plant material contains water and nitrogen and thus will break down faster than dry, withered materials. It's a good idea to add some native soil (a couple of shovels full) to each pile to inoculate the pile with native-soil microorganisms. To thrive, microorganisms need (1) an energy source, which is any carbon material such as leaves or wood (2) a nitrogen source such as manure, green foliage, or organic fertilizers (3) vitamins, which are stored in most living tissue, and (4) moisture.

Watering the pile thoroughly is important and best done while mixing the

Compost—Mother Nature's Fertilizer

original ingredients together. The proper moisture level is between 40-50%, similar to the wetness of a squeezed-out sponge. Piles that are too wet will be anaerobic and not decay properly. Piles that are too dry won't compost properly or fast enough. Once you have gotten the pile evenly moist, it's easy to keep it there. Give it a little water during dry periods. If you have ants in your compost pile, it's too dry.

Turning the pile is important. Turning keeps the mixture aerobic by helping oxygen penetrate the material. Turning also ensures that all the ingredients are exposed to the beneficial fungi, bacteria, and other microorganisms that work to break the raw material down into humus. It also ensures that all the ingredients are exposed to the cleansing heat of the center of the pile. In a properly "cooking" compost pile, the heat of approximately 150° kills the weed seed and harmful pathogens but stimulates the beneficial microorganisms. Don't be concerned if your pile heats for a while and then cools off—that's natural. The entire process takes anywhere from 2 months to a year depending on how often the pile is turned. If the ingredients contain a high percentage of wood chips, the process may take even longer. It's interesting that softwood sawdust and chips break down more slowly than hardwood.

Compost activators are beneficial in getting the pile to heat up and cook faster. Although most any organic fertilizer can be used as a compost activator, they should be mixed into the pile at 3-4 lbs./cu. yd. of compost.

Compost can be used in many ways. Partially completed compost makes a very effective top-dressing mulch for ornamental or vegetable gardens. It's easy to tell when the compost is finished and ready to use as a fertilizer and soil amendment. The original material will no longer be identifiable, the texture will be soft and crumbly, and the fragrance will be rich and earthy.

Compost can be used to fertilize grass areas, planting beds, vegetable gardens, and potted plants. It is the only material I recommend for the preparation of new planting beds. Why is compost better than pine bark or peat moss? Because it's alive, and those other materials are not.

APPENDIX

APPENDIX

CONVERSION TABLES: CHEMICAL MIXING CHART AND RECIPES

U se this table to determine the amount of liquid/dry chemicals to add to water based on a standard of a given amount per 100 gallons in the manufacturer's instructions. Example: If the manufacturer recommends 8 oz. per 100 gallons, and 1 gallon of mix is required, read the table from left to right, 8 oz./100 gallon column over to $^1/_2$ tsp./gallon column.

CHEMICAL MIXING CHART AND RECIPES

Liquid Equivalent Table

100 gal	25 gal	12$^1/_2$ gal	5 gal	1 gal
2 gal	2 qt	1 qt	12$^3/_4$ oz	2$^1/_2$ oz
1 gal	1 qt	1 pt	6$^1/_2$ oz	2$^1/_2$ tbl
2 qts	1 pt	8 oz	3$^1/_4$ oz	3$^3/_4$ tsp
3 pt	12 oz	6 oz	5 tbl	1 tbl
1 qt	$^1/_2$ pt	4 oz	3 tbl	2 tsp
1$^1/_2$ pt	6 oz	3 oz	2$^1/_2$ tbl	1$^1/_2$ tsp
1 pt	4 oz	2 oz	5 tsp	1 tsp
8 oz	2 oz	1 oz	3 tsp	$^1/_2$ tsp

Powder (Dry) Equivalent Table

100 gal	25 gal	12$^1/_2$ gal	5 gal	1 gal
5 lb	1$^1/_4$ lb	12 oz	4 oz	4$^4/_5$ tsp
4 lb	1 lb	8 oz	3$^1/_2$ oz	3$^4/_5$ tsp
3 lb	12 oz	6 oz	2$^3/_8$ oz	2$^4/_5$ tsp
2 lb	8 oz	4 oz	1$^3/_4$ oz	2 tsp
1 lb	4 oz	2 oz	$^7/_8$ oz	1 tsp
8 oz	2 oz	1 oz	$^3/_8$ oz	$^1/_2$ tsp
4 oz	1 oz	$^1/_2$ oz	$^3/_{16}$ oz	$^1/_4$ tsp

1 oz. = 6 tsp. (liq.), 9 tsp. (dry) 1 oz. = 2 tbls. (liq.), 5 tbls .(dry) 1 tbl. = 3 tsp. (liq), 4 tsp. (dry)

APPLICATION RATE CHART

800 lbs./acre	20 lbs./1,000 sq. ft.	
400 lbs./acre	10 lbs./1,000 sq. ft.	
200 lbs./acre	5 lbs./1,000 sq. ft.	
1 qt./acre	2 tbs./1,000 sq. ft.	1 oz./1,000 sq. ft.
13 oz./acre	1 tsp./1,000 sq. ft.	3 oz./1,000 sq. ft.
11 gal./acre	1 qt./1,000 sq. ft.	
400 lbs./acre	10 lbs./1,000 sq. ft.	
250 lbs./acre	6 lbs./1,000 sq. ft.	
1 qt./acre	2 tbs./1,000 sq. ft.	
1 lb./acre	.4 oz./1,000 sq. ft.	
1.5 oz./acre	7 drops/gal./1,000 sq. ft	
13 oz./acre	1 tsp./1,000 sq. ft.	
4 oz./acre	.10 oz./1,000 sq. ft. (30 drops per gal.)	
8 oz./acre	.20 oz./1,000 sq. ft. (60 drops per gal.)	
1 gal./10 acres	13 oz./acre	
1.5 gal. /10 acres	19 oz./acre	
.5 gal. /10 acres	6 oz./acre	
6" soil	2 million lbs./acre	

LINEAR MEASURE

1 foot	12 inches		
1 hand	$1/3$ foot	4 inches	
1 span	9 inches		
1 yard	3 feet		
1 rod	$16^{1/2}$ feet	$5^{1/2}$ yards	
1 furlong	40 poles	220 yards	
1 mile	8 furlongs (1,760 yards)	5,280 feet	320 rods
1 league	3 miles		
1 degree	$69^{1/8}$ miles		

SQUARE OR AREA MEASURE

1 square foot	144 square inches	
1 square yard	9 square feet	
1 acre	160 square rods	43,560 sq. ft.
1 section	640 acres	1 square mile

COMMON MEASUREMENTS

One pinch or dash	$1/16$ teaspoon
1 ounce	360 drops
1 teaspoon	$1/6$ ounce (60 drops)
1 tablespoon	3 teaspoons ($1/2$ ounce liquid, 180 drops)
1 gallon (gal.)	769 teaspoons (256 tablespoons, 128 ounces, 32 cups, 16 pints, 4 quarts)
4 tablespoons	$1/4$ cup (2 ounces liquid)
$1/3$ cup	5 tablespoons plus 1 teaspoon
$1/2$ cup	8 tablespoons (4 ounces liquid)
1 gill	$1/2$ cup (4 ounces liquid)
1 cup	16 tablespoons (8 ounces liquid)
1 pint (pt.)	2 cups (16 ounces liquid)
1 quart (qt.)	2 pints (32 ounces liquid)
4 quarts	1 gallon
1 peck	8 quarts
1 bushel	4 pecks
1 pound	16 ounces (dry measure)
1 barrel (bbl.)	$3 1/2$ gallons
1 acre foot	325,000 gallons

CUBIC OR VOLUME MEASURE (A legal cord of wood is 4 feet high, 4 feet wide, and 8 feet long.)

1 cubic foot	1,728 cubic inches	
1 cubic yard	27 cubic feet	
1 cord of wood	128 cubic feet	
1 board foot	144 cubic inches	1/12 cubic foot

METRIC EQUIVALENTS

Linear

1 millimeter (mm.)	.0394 in.	
1 centimeter (cm.)	.3937 in.	
1 decimeter (dm.)	3.937 in.	
1 meter (m.)	39.37 in.	1.1 yard
1 decameter	393.7 in.	10 yd. 2.8 ft.
1 hectometer	328 ft. 1 in.	
1 kilometer	3,280 ft. 1 in.	

CONVERSIONS

1 sq. yd.	9 sq. ft.
1 cu. yd.	27 cu. ft.

DRY MEASURE

1 quart	2 pints
1 peck	8 quarts
1 bushel (bu.)	4 pecks

COMMON EQUIVALENTS

1 bushel	2,150 cubic inches or $1^1/_4$ cubic feet
1 gallon	231 cubic inches
1 cubic foot	$7^1/_2$ gallons
1 cubic foot of water	$62^1/_2$ pounds (62.43 lb.)
1 gallon of water	$8^1/_3$ pounds (8.345 lb.)
1 cubic foot of ice	$57^1/_2$ pounds

APPLICATION RATES (Bulk material)

(1 cu. ft. =)	(1 cu. yd. =)	(3 cu. ft. bagged)	(2 cu. ft. bagged)
12 sq. ft. 1" deep	1,296 sq. ft. $^1/_4$" deep	36 sq. ft. 1" deep	96 sq. ft. $^1/_4$" deep
6 sq. ft. 2" deep	648 sq. ft. $^1/_2$" deep	18 sq. ft. 2" deep	48 sq. ft. $^1/_2$" deep
4 sq. ft. 3" deep	324 sq. ft. 1" deep	12 sq. ft. 3" deep	24 sq. ft. 1" deep
3 sq. ft. 4" deep	162 sq. ft. 2" deep	9 sq. ft. 4" deep	12 sq. ft. 2" deep
	91 sq. ft. 3" deep		8 sq. ft. 3" deep
	$45^1/_2$ sq. ft. 4" deep		6 sq. ft. 4" deep

CONVERSION TABLES

U.S.		Abbreviations		Metric	
1 teaspoon	60 drops	Teaspoon	t.	1 teaspoon	5 milliliters
1 tablespoon	3 teaspoons	Tablespoon	T.	1 tablespoon	15 milliliters
1 tablespoon	180 drops	Cup	c.	1 ounce	30 milliliters
1 ounce	2 tablespoons	Pint	pt.	1 quart	.940 liters
1 ounce	360 drops	Quart	qt.	1 gallon	3.76 liters
1 cup	8 ounces	Gallon	gal.		
1 pound	16 ounces	Ounce	oz.		
1 pint (16 oz.)	2 cups	Pound	lb.		
1 quart (32 oz.)	2 pints	Milliliter	ml.		
1 gallon (128 oz.)	4 quarts	Liter	l.		
1 gallon	16 cups				
1 gallon	128 ounces				

DILUTION CHART (Gallons of Water)

Dilution	1 Qt.	1 Gal.	3 Gal.	5 Gal.	10 Gal.	15 Gal.
1-10	3 oz.	12 oz.	2¹/₄ pts.	2 qts.	3³/₄ qts.	5¹/₂ qts.
1-50	4 t.	5 T.	7¹/₂ oz.	12¹/₂ oz.	25 oz.	37¹/₂ oz.
1-80	1 T.	2 oz.	6 oz.	10 oz.	20 oz.	30 oz.
1-100	2 t.	2¹/₂ T.	3¹/₂ oz.	6¹/₄ oz.	12¹/₂ oz.	19 oz.
1-200	1 t.	4 t.	2 oz.	3¹/₂ oz.	6¹/₂ oz.	10 oz.
1-400	¹/₂ t.	2 t.	2 T.	1¹/₂ oz.	3 oz.	5 oz.
1-800	—	1 t.	1 T.	5 t.	1¹/₂ oz.	2¹/₂ oz.

SOIL NUTRIENT AVAILABILITY

Nutrient	Low	Normal	High	Very High
Calcium	<20	20-60	60-80	>80
Magnesium	<10	10-25	25-35	>35
Potassium	< 5	5-20	20-30	>30
Phosphorus	<.1	.1-.4	.5-.8	>.8
Nitrogen	< 1	1-10	10-20	>20
Nitrate	< 5	5-50	50-100	>100
Sulfate	<30	30-90	90-180	>180
Sulfur	<10	10-30	30-60	>60

Numbers above represent available percentages in the soil.

PRODUCT RATE CHART

Product	Rate	Frequency/Comments
Alfalfa meal	20 to 25 lbs. per 1,000 sq. ft.	Once a year in conjunction with other organic fertilizers.
Bat guano	10 to 20 lbs. per 1,000 sq. ft.	Once a year to flowering plants or at each flower rotation.
Blood meal	10 to 20 lbs. per 1,000 sq. ft.	May be combined with cottonseed meal (4 parts cottonseed meal to 1 part blood meal).
Bone meal	10 to 20 lbs. per 1,000 sq. ft.	Once a year when planting bulbs or flowers. Watch for calcium buildup.
Chelated Iron	1 qt./acre or 1 tbs./gal.	Spray as needed for a quick temporary fix of iron deficiency.
Cow manure	20 to 30 lbs. per 1,000 sq. ft. up to 5 tons per acre	Use composted manure to avoid weeds; raw material good to use on agricultural fields. Watch for buildup of phosphates and nitrates.
Cottonseed meal	20 to 30 lbs. per 1,000 sq. ft.	Use once or twice a year. May be combined with blood meal or other meals.
Colloidal phosphate	25 to 50 lbs. per 1,000 sq. ft.	Use once per year to give a long-lasting source of phosphorous and calcium. Put small handful into planting hole of new plants.
Compost	1/4-inch depth on lawns; 2-inch depth in beds. 900-1,200 lbs./ac. on agriculture fields	Once a year to lawns and planting beds is ideal. Not important if beds are mulched.
Earthworm castings	10 lbs. per 1,000 sq. ft.	Use once per year or at each annual flower rotation on flowering plants as a supplemental food. Put a small handful in each planting hole.
Epsom salts	1 tbs. per gal.	Spray monthly if needed. Can be mixed with other sprays. For soils deficient in sulfer and magnesium.

Product Rate Chart Continued

Product	Rate	Frequency/Comments
Fish emulsion	2 oz./gal of water per 1,000 sq. ft.	Spray all plants 2 to 3 times per year or any time extra greening or pest control is needed.
Fish meal	20 lbs. per 1,000 sq. ft.	Once or twice a year to lawns or planting beds as a supplemental fertilizer. Use 10 pounds per 1,000 sq. ft. after the first year.
Granite sand	10 lbs. per 1,000 sq. ft. up to 5 tons per acre.	Once a year as a mineral supplement. Can also be used to top-dress new, solid-sod installations.
Greensand	10 to 20 lbs. per 1,000 sq. ft.	Excellent mineral supplement.
Humate (Dry)	$1^1/_2$-5 lbs. per 1,000 sq. ft.	Use high quality humate (40-50° humic acid) @ 50 lbs./acre once per year.
Humate (Liquid)	1-2 oz./1,000 sq. ft.	Spray all foliage lightly 3 times per growing season. Can be mixed with other liquid products.
Hydrogen peroxide (H_2O_2)	$^1/_2$ oz of 35 percent material per gal./1,000 sq. ft. or 8 oz. of 3% material per gal. per 1,000 sq. ft.	Can be mixed with other materials but always add the H_2O_2 first.
Lava sand	10 lbs. per 1,000 sq. ft. up to 5 tons per acre	Once a year as a mineral supplement. Can also be used to top dress new solid sod installations.
Manalfa	800 lbs./acre or 20 lbs./1,000 sq. ft.	10 lbs./1,000 sq. ft. after 1st full year.
Manure on fields	500-1,000 lbs./acre	In the beginning, as much as 5 tons per acre can be used until fertility levels increase.
Molasses	1 oz. per gal. of water or other liquids dry-20 lbs./1,000 s.f.	Apply as a foliar and soil spray to fertilize and feed microbes.

Product Rate Chart Continued

Product	Rate	Frequency/Comments
Organic fertilizers in general	20 lbs./1,000 sq. ft.	1/2 tsp./4" pot, 1 tsp./gal, 1 tbs./5 gal. container. Water in after application.
Poultry manure	20 lbs. per 1,000 sq. ft. the first year; 10 pounds thereafter. Composted only	Apply twice per year as a good natural source of nitrogen.
Seaweed (Liquid kelp)	1/2 to 1 oz. per 1,000 sq. ft.	Apply to lawns and planting beds once a month as a supplement between applications of dry fertilizers.
Seaweed (Kelp meal)	10 to 20 lbs./1,000 sq. ft.	Apply to lawns and planting beds once a month as a supplement between applications of dry fertilizers.
Seaweed and Fish emulsion	Mix 1 oz. of seaweed and 2 oz. of fish emulsion per gallon of water	Apply as a general foliar spray to aid insect and fungus control and as a foliar feed. Spray all plants and lawns.
Soybean meal	20 lbs. per 1,000 sq. ft.	Apply twice per year.
Sul-Po-Mag	20 lbs. per 1,000 sq. ft.	Use once per year on soil needing sulfur, magnesium, and potassium.
Vinegar	1/2 oz. per gal.	Mix with other liquid products use 1 to 2 gal. of mix per 1,000 sq. ft.

HOMEMADE SOLUTIONS

PHARAOH ANT BAIT
(Sugar Ants)
1 teaspoon of creamy peanut butter
1 pat of butter or oleo
1 tablespoon of any light syrup
1 teaspoon of boric acid powder

Blend the above ingredients over low heat until smooth—be careful not to burn the solution. Put the finished bait into lids or other small containers. The ants will find them. This amount will make several bait stations—feed ants as long as they will take the bait. Do not use this recipe on your waffles or pancakes. Remember that boric acid is poison. Change the sweet ingredients from time to time to prevent the ants from catching on.

ROACH CONTROL
(Mom called 'em water bugs)

1 Eliminate the food and water sources. Fix dripping faucets and leaky pipes. Do not leave dirty dishes, food scraps, pet food, or any other tasty morsels out for the bugs to snack on.

2 Plug any holes or cracks where roaches can gain access to the house. Steel wool can be used to fill voids around pipes, etc.

3 Apply a light dusting of boric acid to areas such as behind and between appliances where roaches like to party. For additional control, mix pyrethrum and diatomaceous earth together with the boric acid. Use *light* dustings. If the material can be seen after application, you probably put out too much.

4 For even more control, make a bait by mixing 2 parts boric acid, 1 part sugar, and enough water to create little cakes. Put the cakes behind appliances where roaches hide. An even less toxic bait can be made by mixing Arm and Hammer detergent together in a 50-50 mix with sugar.

FLEA CONTROL
If you are ready to stop dumping toxic chemicals on your lawn, gardens, carpets, furniture, pets, and yourself, here's my holistic flea program:

1 **DIET:** Feed pets a balanced, nutritious diet of your own cooking or an organic pet food such as Pro Plan Turkey & Barley Formula. Sprinkle a small amount of garlic powder or a crushed garlic clove and raw diatomaceous earth (1% or less) on the pet food daily.

2 **CLEANING:** Vacuum frequently, rake and sweep dog runs and sleeping areas regularly, pick up and compost pet waste.

3 **EXERCISE:** If the pets don't get natural exercise from running and playing, walk them regularly. It's good for the animals and for you.

4 **GROOMING:** Bathe pets as needed but only with mild, nontoxic soaps like Shaklee's shampoo or Neo-Life soap. Herbal shampoos are good, also Dr. Bronners Eucalyptus Soap. Leave shampoo on pet for 5 minutes before rinsing. Brush pets regularly and use a flea comb to remove pests. Drown them in soapy water—the fleas, not the pets.

5 **OUTDOOR TREATMENTS:** Dust or spray diatomaceous earth and pyrethrum on infested areas. Light dusting is better

than heavy amounts. In liquid sprays, add 2 tablespoons D.E./pyrethrum to 1 gallon of water. Use only as needed to avoid killing beneficial insects.

6 **INDOOR TREATMENT:** Sprinkle salt on carpets. Work in and leave overnight to dehydrate fleas. Vacuum the next day. Mix salt, diatomaceous earth, and boric acid together (1/3 each) for more power. For heavy infestations, spray d-limonene (Demize or Flea Stop) and methoprene (Precor or Ovitrol) on carpets and furniture.

7 **PET TREATMENT:** Apply herbal powders of pennyroyal, eucalyptus, or rosemary. Treat heavy infestations with D.E./pyrethrum products; ready-to-use growth regulator products such as Petcor and Ovitrol are also available.

Note: Remember, D.E. (diatomaceous earth) for pets and pests is not the same as swimming pool D.E. Buy D.E. only from your local organic retailer.

FIRE ANTS
First of all, go organic and encourage biodiversity. Treat large-scale infestations with Logic or Award 1 lb./ac. on a dry day. Make sure the ants are foraging by putting out a piece of chicken or some jelly. Knock out individual problem mounds by pouring into the center of the mound one of the following: strong vinegar with diatomaceous earth or a pyrethrum/rotenone product. Avoid products that contain chemical solvents. Individual mounds can also be knocked out with dry D.E./pyrethrum powder or soapy water.

GARLIC/PEPPER TEA
Garlic/pepper tea—liquify 2 bulbs of garlic and 2 cayenne or habenero peppers in a blender ¹/₃ full of water. Strain the solids out and add enough water to the garlic/pepper juice to make 1 gallon of concentrate. Shake well before using and add ¹/₄ cup of the concentrate to each gallon of water in the sprayer. 2 tablespoons of vegetable oil per gallon of concentrate will make the tea stronger but I doubt it's needed. *Do not store home brews in glass. The gases can expand and cause the glass to explode. Use plastic.*

GARLIC FLY KILLER
Recycle the pulp from the garlic tea preparation by adding some water to solids and set it outside—several feet from the back door. It not only attracts flies but *kills* them in the process. Later, toss it in the compost pile.

REPELLENT FOR PETS, RABBITS, AND SQUIRRELS
Dog-B-Gone—1 part cayenne pepper, 1 part dry mustard powder, 2 parts flour. Sprinkle on top of ground. Don't water in! Rover will quit going there eventually and mark other territory, and you will no longer need to treat original area. Will need to re-treat if there is rain. Cayenne pepper by itself usually works. Habenero works even better.

FLEA BATH
For fleas in the house, use a camera tripod and hang a 40-watt light bulb directly over a pan of soapy water. The fleas go for the light, end up in the soapy water, and drown.

INTERIOR ANT CONTROL
Crushed or chopped pieces of tansy leaf

or bay leaf will repel ants quite effectively. A light dusting of pyrethrum is also very effective.

BEER TRAPS
For slug, snail, and pill bug infestations, pour a small amount of cheap, stale beer (drink the good, cold beer) into a small dish or buried plastic cup. Clean out daily and refill as long as problem persists. A tablespoon of brewer's yeast in water also works.

Note: Keep insecticides away from children and pets. Don't breath the dust of any dusty products. And remember that anything chemical or organic can injure or can kill if mishandled—there is no such thing as nontoxic.

RESOURCES

PUBLICATIONS

A Field Guide To Texas Snakes by Alan Tennant is the best basic guide for snakes found in Texas. Gulf Publishing Company

A Field Guide To Texas Trees by Benny Simpson is a very complete book and an excellent tool for Texas tree identification. Texas Monthly Press

Acres USA Primer by Charles Walters is one of the best overall guides on organics.

Agriculture Testament and *Soil and Health* by Sir Alfred Howard. These state-of-the-art guides to organics and using compost to bring soil back to health were written in the 1940s, but are still two of the best publications on the market. Oxford and Rodale Press

Birder's Guide to Texas by Edward A. Kutac is a good basic guide for birds in Texas. Gulf Publishing Company

Birds of Texas by Roger Tory Peterson is another good guide to birds found in Texas. Houghton Mifflin Company

Bread from Stones by Julius Hensel is a classic explaining the role of earth minerals in the production of wholesome food crops. Acres U.S.A.

Common Sense Pest Control by William Olkowski, Shiela Daar, Helga Olkowski is an excellent reference for low toxicity pest control. The Taunton Press

Fertile Soil by Robert Parnes, Ph.D. is a book on soil chemistry and fertility.

Growing Fruits, Berries & Nuts Southwest—Southeast by Dr. George Ray McEachern is an excellent book on selecting and growing pecans, fruit trees, and berry plants. Gulf Publishing Company

How To Grow Native Plants of Texas and the Southwest by Jill Nokes is the best book available on propagation of native Texas plants. Texas Monthly Press

How to Have a Green Thumb Without an Aching Back, Exposition Press, *Gardening Without Work,* Devin-Adair, and *The No Work Gardening Book,* Rodale Press, by Ruth Stout are great. She was a humorous writer, a philosopher, and an advocate of mulching. They are hard to find as are Sir Alfred Howard's books, but the Tracery in Dallas can usually track them down for you.

How to Heal the Earth in Your Spare Time by Andrew Lopez is an excellent guide to homemade organic solutions. Acres U.S.A.

Introduction To Soil Microbiology, second edition , by Martin Alexander. John Wiley & Sons

Know It and Grow It II by Dr. Carl Whitcomb is an excellent general reference for plant materials of the South. Lacebark Press

Landscape Design...Texas Style by Howard Garrett. This book is a well-kept secret about my design and landscape philosophy as well as a rather decent reference book on landscape construction and regional plant material selection. Out of print but can be found in libraries.

Let It Rot by Stu Campbell explains the art of composting in clear and easy-to-read instructions. This is the best book on composting I have found. Garden Way Publishing

Native Texas Plants—Landscaping Region by Region by Sally and Andy Wasowski is an excellent tool for use in selecting and using native Texas plant materials. Gulf Publishing Company

Natural Insect Repellents for Pets and People by Connie Moore and Janette Grainger is a clear and simple guide to using herbs and other organic techniques for pet care. Published by The Herb Bar

Nature's Silent Music by Dr. Phil Callahan explains how to preserve the health of the land by avoiding toxic chemicals and working within nature's laws and systems. Acres U.S.A.

Odena's Texas Herb Book, Lavender Hill Cook Book, Little Sprout (for children), *Saffron: Spice of Kings* by Odena G. Brannam. Lavender Hill Herb Farm, 503 Mill Street, Ladonia, Texas 75449

Organic Gardening Magazine 33 E. Minor St. Emmaus, PA 18098. The oldest reference on organic gardening. Joe and Robert Rodale are both now dead but their book and inspiration live on.

Perennial Garden Color by Dr. William C. Welch is the best basic guide for the selection and use of perennials in Texas. Taylor Publishing

Plants Of The Metroplex III by J. Howard Garrett covers organic planting techniques and the recommended trees, shrubs, ground covers, vines, herbs, and flowers of Texas. Lantana Publishing

Rodale's Color Handbook of Garden Insects by Anna Carr is a field guide of practical information for gardeners, farmers, and homeowners.

Rodale's Garden Problem Solver by Jim Ball addresses more than 700 specific gardening problems and answers thousands of general gardening questions on insect and animal pests, weeds, propagation, and diseases.

Roses Love Garlic and *Carrots Love Tomatoes* both by Louise Riotte. *Carrots Love Tomatoes* shows you how to arrange your garden for the most complementary relationships. Topics included are flower and vegetable interplanting, plants that deter insects and diseases, and planting to keep weeds down. *Roses Love Garlic* explains companion planting with flowers. It tells you how to combine flower and vegetable gardens, introduces you to many unique plants, and explains how to use them. Garden Way Publishing

Science in Agriculture by Dr. Arden Anderson is a "must have" and "must study" book for anyone interested in eco-agriculture. Acres U.S.A.

Seaweed and Plant Growth by Dr. T. L. Senn explains in detail the wonderful powers of seaweed as a fertilizer and root stimulator. It explains how seaweed can be used as a supplement to the fertilization program to improve plant resistance to stress of all kinds, including cold tolerance. Senn

Shepherd's Purse Organic Pest Control Book is available through The Book Publishing Company in Summertown, Tennessee. It is an excellent book on organic insect control.

Silent Spring by Rachel Carson. If you don't convert to organics after reading this classic, you never will. The Riverside Press, Cambridge

Soil Fertility by Robert Parnes, Ph.D., is a comprehensive technical reference manual that explains using a non-chemical fertilizer program to create and maintain healthy, balanced soil.

Southern Herb Growing by Madalene Hill and Gwen Barclay is a good book on general herb growing. It includes color photos, cultural needs, and uses of over 130 herbs. It also contains recipes. Shearer Publishing

The Albrecht Papers by William Albrecht, which are a compilation of papers by the late Dr. Albrecht and are the bible for managing soil health.

The Basic Book of Organic Gardening by Rodale includes the definition of an organic gardener, the secrets of the best organic gardeners, alternatives to insecticides, and vegetable gardening information.

The Bug Book by John and Helen Philbrick is an excellent, little reference book on organic insect control with emphasis on how to take advan-

tage of beneficial bugs. Garden Way Publishing

The Chemical Free Lawn Care by Warren Shultz is a book offering detailed information on how to establish and maintain lawns using organic techniques. It's a well-written and easy-to-follow book on non-toxic alternatives. Rodale

The Complete Guide to Texas Lawn Care by Dr. William E. Knoop is a very thorough turf reference book for the South. T G Press

The Encyclopedia of Natural Insect & Disease Control is a comprehensive reference on controlling insects and diseases in the garden, orchard, and yard without chemicals. Rodale

The Encyclopedia of Organic Gardening is a comprehensive book covering everything from bee keeping to vegetables, including information on nearly 700 fruits, flowers, vegetables, and ornamentals. Rodale

The Garden-Ville Method (Lessons in Nature) is written by my mentor and the king of compost, Malcolm Beck, one of the most knowledgeable people on organics in the country. Beck

The Herb Garden Cookbook by Lucinda Hutson is not only a great cookbook but also has excellent basic information on the culture of herbs. Gulf Publishing Company

The One—Straw Revolution by Masanoku Fukuoka is a wonderful introductory book to natural farming. Rodale Press

The Secret Garden by Frances Hodgson Burnett. For children of all ages, this delightful book introduces the reader to the magic of nature. Knopf

The Soul of the Ghost Moth by Dr. Phil Callahan explains why insects are attracted to plants. Acres U.S.A.

The Soul of the Soil by Grace Gershuny and Joseph Smillie is a little book that's a nice guide to ecological soil management. GAIA Services

The Vegetable Book by Dr. Sam Cotner is quite simply the best nonorganic book available on growing veggies in Texas. T G Press

Weeds by Charles Walters. A thorough review and explanation of how to control weeds through soil management. Acres U.S.A.

GENERAL SOURCES

Acres U.S.A—A monthly newspaper that covers organic agriculture, ecological farming, and bio-dynamics. P. O. Box 9547, Kansas City, MO 64133. 816-737-0064.

Bat Conservancy International—P. O. Box 162063, Austin, TX 78716. Merlin Tuttle, Bert Grantges.

Bio-Integral Resource Center (B.I.R.C.)—Box 7414, Berkeley, CA 94707. This is the source of legitimate Integrated Pest Management information. Other groups and institutions have often misused the term.

Gardens Alive—A quarterly magazine

and mail-order catalog for organic techniques and products. Natural Gardening Research Center, Hwy 48 —P. O. Box 149, Sunman, IN 47041.

Holistic Resource Management—an international, nonprofit organization helping people learn how to stop the desertification of the planet. Alan Savory is the founder and he and his staff teach regular courses on holistic management. P. O. Box 7128, Albuquerque, NM 87194. 1-800-654-3619.

National Wildflower Research Center—A nonprofit organization dedicated to the re-establishment of native vegetation in Texas. 2600 FM 973 North, Austin, TX 78725. 512-929-3600.

Native Plant Society of Texas—Box 891, Georgetown, TX 78626.

Natural Food Associates—P. O. Box 210, Atlanta, TX 75551. 1-800-594-2136

Rodale Press—Publishers and editors of many books on organics and related subjects including the monthly magazine *Organic Gardening*. 33 East Minor Street, Emmaus, PA 18098.

Sante Fe Natural Tobacco Company—Source of organically grown tobacco. P. O. Box 1840, Sante Fe, NM.

Seeds of Change—Catalog for open-pollinated seed. 505-535-2255, P. O. Box 280, Gila, NM 88038.

Seed Saver Exchange—(Seeds) 319-382-5990. Kent Wheely, Rt. 3 Box 239, Decorah, IA 52101.

Stockman Grass Farmer—P. O. Box 9607, Jackson, MS 39286-9909.

Ronniger Seed Potatoes—Route 3, Moyle Springs, ID 83845. Organically grown seed potatoes, $1.00 for catalog.

Turner Seed Company—(Native Seed) Route 1, Box 292, Breckenridge, TX 76024. 1-800-722-8616.

ORGANIC GROWERS AND SUPPLIERS

Arbico—(Beneficial insects) P. O. Box 4247, Tuscon, AZ 85738. 800-827-2847.

Biofac—(Beneficial insects) 512-547-3259, P. O. Box 87, Mathis, TX 78368.

Bio Insect Control—(Beneficial insects) 806-293-5861, 710 S. Columbia, Plainview, Texas 79072.

Biome—P. O. Box 6706, Katy, TX 77491-6706.

Biosys—(Organic products) 415-856-9500, 1057 E. Meadow Circle, Palo Alto, CA 94303.

Blue Cottage Herb Farm—(Herbs) 903-498-4234, Rt. 1 Box 1075 Kaufman, TX 75142.

Burpee Seed Company—215-674-4900, 300 Park Avenue, Warminster, PA 18974.

Herbal Gems—(Herbs) 214-876-2130, Box 775, Frankston, TX 75763.

Integrated Pest Management—818-287-1101, 305 Agostino Road, San Gabriel, CA 91776.

Johnston Seed Co.—(Native Seed) P. O. Box 1392, 411 West Chestnut, Enid, OK 73702.

Lavender Hill Herb Farm—(Herbs) 214-391-1030, 8755 Quinn, Dallas, TX 75227.

M & R Durango—(Beneficial insects) 800-526-4075, P. O. Box 886, Bayfield, CO 81122.

Mellinger's Nursery—(Organic products) 800-321-7444, 2310 W. South Range Road, North Lima, OH 44452, organic fertilizers, pesticides, seeds, beneficial insects.

Native American Seed Co.—(Buffalograss and wildflower seed) 214-539-0534, 3400 Long Prairie, Flower Mound, TX 75028.

Natural Gardening Research Ctr.—(Organic products) 812-623-3800, P. O. Box 149, Sunman, IN 47041.

Nature's Control—(Organic products) 503-899-8318, P. O. Box 35, Medford, OR 97501.

Necessary Trading Co.—(Organic farming products) 703-864-5103, P. O. Box 603, New Castle, VA 24127.

OrCon, Inc.—(Beneficial insects) 213-937-7444, 5132 Venice Blvd., Los Angeles, CA 90019.

Organic Cotton Pillows and Furniture—825 Northlake Dr., Richardson, TX 75080. Dona Shrier, 214-235-0485.

Organic Pest Management—(Beneficial insects) 206-367-0707, P. O. Box 55267, Seattle, WA 98155.

Peaceable Kingdom School—Old River Road, Washington, TX 77880. Classes on organic techniques. 409-878-2353.

Peaceful Valley Farm Supply—11173 Peaceful Valley Rd., Nevada City, CA 95959. 916-265-3276. Mail order pest controls, organic fertilizers, nursery stock, seeds, tools and consulting.

Pest Management Services—(Beneficial insects) Rt. 12 Box 346-31, Lubbock, TX 79424.

Rincon-Vitova Insectaries—(Beneficial insects) 800-248-BUGS, P. O. Box 95, Oak View, CA 93022.

Southern Exposure Seed—(Heritage seed) P. O. Box 158, North Garden, VA 22959. 804-973-4703.

The Organic Products, Books—29169 Healthercliff Road, #216-408, Malibu, CA 90265. 213-457-1893.

The Orchard (Organic Orchard)—214-771-2097, Rt. 2 Box 22 A, Rockwall, TX 75087.

GLOSSARY

GLOSSARY

ACID CATIONS: A cation that tends to increase soil acidity. In practice, aluminum and hydrogen are the only significant acid cations.

ACID SOIL: Soils with a pH less than 7. If the pH is near 6, a soil is considered slightly or moderately acid; if below 5.5, it is very acid.

AERATION: A mechanical process of punching holes, used to relieve the effects of soil compaction.

AEROBIC: An environment containing oxygen. In the soil, aerobic conditions favor organisms that oxidize organic residues and produce carbon dioxide as a major byproduct.

AGRISPON: A mineral and plant-extract product that stimulates microorganisms and basic soil and plant functions. Manufactured in Texas by Appropriate Technologies.

ALKALINE SOIL: Soils with a pH greater than 7.

AMINO ACIDS: The building blocks of proteins. They are made primarily from nitrogen and carbohydrates, but many also contain sulfur, phosphorous, and other minerals.

AMMONIUM NITRATE: 33-0-0 (NH_4NO_3) A water soluble chemical compound containing approximately 33.5% nitrogen, one half of which is in the ammonia form and one half in the nitrate form.

AMMONIUM PHOSPHATE: A solid fertilizer material manufactured by reacting ammonia with phosphoric acid.

AMMONIUM SULFATE: 21-0-0 ($(NH_4)_2SO_4$) A solid material manufactured by reacting ammonia with sulfuric acid.

ANAEROBIC: Without oxygen. Anaerobic decomposition is less efficient than aerobic organisms. Nitrogen fixation by free-living organisms usually occurs under anaerobic conditions.

ANHYDROUS AMMONIA: 82-0-0 (NH_3) A gas containing approximately 82% nitrogen. Under pressure, ammonia gas is changed to a liquid and usually is stored and transported in this form. Anhydrous ammonia is used to make most of the solid forms of nitrogenous fertilizers and also is used for direct application to the soil either as a gas or in the form of aqua ammonia. The most soil-destructive fertilizer in the world.

ANION: An ion with a negative electrical charge. Sulfur, phosphorous, boron, chlorine, and molybdenum exist in the soil as anions.

ANION EXCHANGE: A condition, analogous to cation exchange, where one anion can replace another at the surface of a clay mineral.

ANTIDESICCANTS: Liquid sprays used to coat the foliage of plants for the purpose of reducing transpiration in hot weather and increasing cold tolerance in winter.

BACILLUS THURINGIENSIS (Bt): Biological insecticides that specifically target caterpillars and other problem insects.

BANDING FERTILIZER: The process of spreading fertilizer in bands rather than broadcasting it. The fertilizer may be spread along a line about two inches to the side of a planted seed and sometimes two inches below. It is considered one of the best methods for utilizing commercial soluble fertilizers, especially phosphorous.

BASE CATIONS: a cation that tends to increase the soil pH. In practice the term is restricted to calcium, magnesium, and potassium.

BAT GUANO: Bat poop.

BIODIVERSITY: Biodiversity of life is not just important, it's critical. The outstanding characteristics of nature are variety and dynamic stability. A healthy situation exists when we create ranches, farms, gardens, and landscapes that have a complex mix of microorganisms, insects, animals, and plants. To understand nature is to grasp the concept that nature is a whole and can't be subdivided. Everything relates to everything else.

BLOOD MEAL: A dry, organic fertilizer made of the blood from slaughterhouses. Normal analysis will be approximately 12-0-0.

BONE MEAL: Cooked bones ground to a meal without any of the gelatin or glue removed. Steamed bone meal has been steamed under pressure to dissolve and remove part of the gelatin.

BORAX: ($Na_2B_4O_7 \bullet 10H_2O$) A salt (sodium borate) used in fertilizer as a source of the minor plant-food element boron. Borax contains about 11% of the element boron. It is available in food stores and is a suitable fertilizer for supplying boron.

BORDEAUX MIX: A fungicide and insecticide made by mixing solutions of copper sulfate and lime, or of copper arsenate and phenols. Use the first one.

BUFFER CAPACITY: The degree to which a substance can resist changes in its characteristics.

BURNED LIME: Limestone heated to

drive out carbon dioxide. Same as quick-lime.

CALCAREOUS: Containing calcium or calcian carbonate.

CALCITE: Limestone containing mostly calcium carbonate, $CaCO_3$. A more common name is ground agricultural limestone.

CALCIUM CARBONATE: ($CaCo_3$) The principal component of calcitic limestone and one of the principal components of dolomitic limestone, of which magnesium carbonate, $MgCO_3$ is the other. Marl and oyster shells also are composed primarily of calcium carbonate.

CARBOHYDRATES: Stabilized structures of sugars. Carbohydrates form the skeleton of the plant, and they are a means for storing energy for a long period of time.

CATION: An ion with a positive electrical charge. Calcium, magnesium, potassium, copper, iron, manganese, and zinc exist in the soil as cations. Nitrogen may be present either as a cation (ammonium) or as an anion (nitrate).

CATION EXCHANGE: A process in which the small number of cations dissolved in the soil water (soluble cations) change place with the much larger number of cations associated with the soil micelles (exchangeable cations).

CATION EXCHANGE CAPACITY: A measure of the ability of the soil components to attract cations and hold them in exchangeable form. The ex-change capacity depends upon the amount of clay, the type of clay, the organic content, and the degree of humification of the organic matter.

CEC: An abbreviation for cation exchange capacity.

CYTOKININ: A plant hormone that can modify plant development by stimulating or altering the cellular RNA.

CHELATION: The chemical process by which an organic substance binds a cation having more than one electrical charge. Chelation is similar to cation exchange. Cation exchange holds the majority of the major cation nutrients (calcium, magnesium, potassium), while chelation holds the cation trace elements (copper, iron, manganese, zinc).

CLIPPINGS: Leaves cut off by mowing.

C/N RATIO: An abbreviation for carbon/nitrogen ratio.

COLLOIDAL: A state of matter where finely divided particles of one substance are suspended in another.

COLLOIDAL PHOSPHATE: Waste material from rock-phosphate mining operation. An excellent, slow-release source of phosphorous, calcium, and trace elements.

COMPACTION: The pressing together of soil particles by foot or vehicular traffic.

COMPANION PLANTING: Using different plants together that assist one another with insect and disease control.

COMPOST: Nature's fertilizer created by the rotting of vegetable and animal matter.

COMPOSTED MANURE: Animal manure that has been taken through the process of natural composting in order to kill pathogens and weed seed.

COOL-SEASON TURFGRASS: Those turfgrasses primarily used in the northern United States, such as Kentucky bluegrass, tall fescue, and ryegrass.

COPPERAS: ($FeSO_4 \bullet 7H_2O$) Ferrous (iron) sulfate used as a trace nutrient fertilizer, especially in alkaline soils.

COPPER SULFATE: ($CuSO_4 \bullet 5H_2O$) Most common source of copper for fertilizer. Also used as an insecticide and fungicide. A common name is blue vitriol.

COTTONSEED MEAL: Fertilizer meal made from ground cottonseed.

COVER CROP: A crop that improves the soil on which it is grown. Many plants are sown primarily as cover crops to cover the ground, improve it, and protect it for a succeeding cash crop. Other plants, such as alfalfa, clover, and most grass-legume sods, can serve as both a cash crop and a cover crop.

CROSS-POLLINATE: To apply pollen of a male flower to the stigma or female part of another flower.

CURCULIO, PLUM: Worm that attacks the fruit of plums and other orchard trees.

CUTTING HEIGHT: The distance between the ground and the blades of the mower.

DAMPING OFF: A disease of seeds and young seedlings caused by fungi.

DENITRIFICATION: The conversion of nitrates in the soil to some form of gaseous nitrogen, which escapes into the atmosphere and is lost.

DIACIDE: Organic insecticide made primarily from diatomaceous earth and natural pyrethrum.

DIAMMONIUM PHOSPHATE: (21-53-0) A solid fertilizer material made by reacting ammonia with phosphoric acid.

DIATOMACEOUS EARTH: An off-white dust from skeletal remains of diatoms. Used as an insecticide and food supplement. Diatomaceous earth or D.E. is very absorptive and abrasive.

DICOTYLEDON (DICOT): A plant with two seed leaves.

DIOECIOUS: Plants that have the male reproductive system on one plant and the female on another.

DNA: (Deoxyribonucleic acid) Nucleic acid found in all living cells.

DOLOMITE: A material used for liming soils in areas where magnesium as well as calcium are needed. Made by grinding dolomitic limestone, which contains both magnesium carbonate, $MgCO_3$, and calcium carbonate, $CaCO_3$.

DORMANT OIL: Petroleum-based oil used for smothering overwinter insects such as scale.

DORMANT TURF: A brown-colored turf that has temporarily ceased growth due to unfavorable environmental conditions.

EARTHWORM CASTINGS: Earthworm poop.

EPIPHYTIC: Referring to plants growing without soil and receiving their nutrients from the air.

EPSOM SALTS: Magnesium sulfate. It is used as a fast-acting source of magnesium and sulfur. Normally used as a foliar feed.

EXCHANGEABLE CATIONS: Those cations that are electrostatically attracted to soil particles. The sum of the exchangeable cations and the soluble cations is considered to constitute the available cations for plant take-up.

FERTIGATION: The application of fertilizer through an irrigation system.

FERTILAID: An organic fertilizer made from slaughterhouse waste such as bone meal, blood meal. Product claims to contain living microorganisms. (4-2-0).

FERTILIZER: Any material or mixture used to supply one or more soil or plant nutrients.

FISH EMULSION: An oily liquid fertilizer made from fish waste or whole fish.

FLOWERS OF SULFUR: Finely granulated sulfur dust, used to acidify an alkaline soil.

FOLIAR BURN: An injury to the leaves of the plant, caused by the application of a fertilizer or pesticide.

FOLIAR SPRAY: Liquid plant nutrients applied by spraying on the foliage.

FOOTPRINTING: Discolored areas, or impressions, left in the lawn from foot traffic when the turf is in the first stage of wilt.

FRENCH DRAIN: A drainage device in which a hole or trench is backfilled with sand or gravel.

FUNGICIDE: A product used to control diseases caused by fungi.

GEOTROPISM: The effect of gravity on plants.

GRANITE SAND: Sand made from weathered or ground-up granite rock.

GREENSAND: A material called glauconite, which is a naturally deposited, undersea, iron-potassium silicate. It's an excellent source of potash with a normal analysis of 0-1-5. It's best used with other fertilizers.

GREEN MANURE: A cover crop used to smother weeds, to protect the soil, and to hold nutrients that might otherwise be leached. Traditionally a green manure is planted after the harvest of a cash crop, but an alternative is a "living mulch," where a cover crop is sown before harvesting the cash crop.

GUANO: Decomposed, dried excrement of birds and bats. Used for fertilizer purposes. The most commonly known guano comes from islands off the coast of Peru and is derived from the excrement of sea fowl. It is high in nitrogen and phosphate, and at one time was a major fertilizer in this country.

GUMOSIS: Stress-related gumming of the vessels in fruit trees. Sometimes caused by the chloride in (KCL) potassium chloride. Potassium sulfate (KSO_4) will not cause the problem.

GYPSUM: ($CaSO_4 2H_2O$) The common name for calcium sulfate, a mineral used in the fertilizer industry as a source of calcium and sulfur. It is a good source of sulfur and is also used to improve alkaline soils having a high sodium content.

HAY: Grass, clover, or the like that is cut while still green and used as a fodder or mulch.

HERBICIDE: A product used for weed control.

HUMUS: The Latin word for soil or earth. It is the broken-down form of organic matter.

HYDROGEN PEROXIDE: (H_2O_2) An oxygenating compound used for soil conditioning and bacteria fighting.

HYDROMULCHING: A method of seeding using a mixture of seed, fertilizer, and mulch, sprayed in a solution on the soil surface.

HYDROSEEDING: Same as hydromulching but without the mulch.

HYDROSPRIGGING: Same as hydromulching but uses sprigs instead of seed.

ION: An electrostatically charged atom formed when a salt is dissolved in water. The dissolved salt breaks up into both positively and negatively charged ions.

IONIC CHARGE: The electrical charge associated with ions. Cations have a positive electrical charge and anions a negative charge.

INSECTICIDE: A product used to control insects.

INTEGRATED PEST MANAGEMENT: Buzz word for using a little bit of organics and a varying bit of chemicals.

IRRIGATION, AUTOMATIC: An irrigation system using preset timing devices.

LANGBEINITE: Sul-Po-Mag

LAYERING, SOIL: An undesirable stratification of a soil.

LEACHING : The movement (usually loss) of dissolved nutrients as water percolates through the soil.

LEATHER TANKAGE: Waste from the leather tanning industry.

LIME: Technically, lime is calcium oxide. In agricultural usage, however, the term is used to denote any liming material.

LIME SULFUR: Organic pesticide used for disease control.

LOCALIZED DRY SPOT: An area of soil that resists wetting.

MAGNESIA: Magnesium oxide, used as an emergency source of magnesium.

MAGNESIUM SULFATE: ($MgSO_4 H_2O$) A soluble salt used as a source of magnesium. Common forms are the mineral kieserite and epsom salts.

MANALFA: Organic fertilizer made from a blend of livestock manure and alfalfa.

MANGANESE SULFATE: $(MnSO_4\text{-}H_2O)$ A solid chemical compound used as a source of manganese for plants.

MANURE: Manure most commonly refers to animal dung, but the term is also used in association with green manuring.

Meq/100 g: The unit of measure of cation exchange capacity and exchangeable cations. It is shorthand for "milliequivalents of exchangeable cations per 100 grams of soil." A milli-equivalent is 1/100 of an equivalent, and an equivalent is the quantity of a cation which will exchange with one gram of hydrogen ions.

MICELLE: Shorthand for micro-cell, it refers to a colloidal clay or humus particle with many negative electrical charges. It attracts positively charged cations.

MILORGANITE: Sewer sludge fertilizer from Milwaukee.

MINERAL OIL: Oil made from refined petroleum products.

MOLYBDENUM: One of the essential micronutrients.

MONOAMMONIUM SULFATE: Synthetic fertilizer containing phosphorous, sulfur, and ammonia. 11-48-0.

MONOECIOUS: Plants that have male and female flowers on the same plant.

MONOVALENT: An ion, either an anion or cation, carrying a single electrical charge.

MULTIVALENT: An ion carrying more than one electrical charge. Chelation can only bind multivalent cations.

MURIATE OF POTASH: (KCl) The principal source of potassium for synthetic fertilizer. Potassium chloride, usually sold on the basis of a material containing 95%-99% KCl, with a K2O equivalent of 60%-62%.

MYCORRHIZAE: Fungi that penetrates roots of plants to extract carbohydrates. Its unique value is that in return it passes mineral nutrients to the plant. It can be a major source of available phosphorus. It is similar to the rhizobia bacteria that inhabit legume roots and fix nitrogen.

NECTAR: A sweet liquid secreted by plants. The main raw material of honey.

NEMATODES: Small hair-like organisms that attack root systems and other soil-borne organisms.

NITRATE INHIBITORS: Substances that retard the ability of soil organisms to transform ammonium to nitrates. Their purpose is to avoid the denitrification which occurs with heavy fertilizer applications of urea, ammonium salts, or liquid ammonia.

NITRATE OF SODA: Sodium nitrate $(NaNO_3)$ A fertilizer material containing approximately 16% nitrogen. The principal source of sodium nitrate has been the natural deposits of the salt in Chile. It is also produced synthetically.

NITRIFICATION: A process which

takes place in the soil whereby soil microorganisms form nitrates from organic matter and the ammonia forms of nitrogen.

NPK: A shorthand notation for "Nitrogen-Phosphate-Potash."

OPEN POLLINATED: Unlike hybrids, plants that will return true from seed.

ORGANIC MATTER: Organic substances in differing stages of decay, varying from litter to very stable humus.

OVERSEEDING: Seeding a dormant turf with a cool-season grass in order to provide color during the winter.

PARTHENOCARPIC: Organisms that don't need to be pollinated to reproduce.

PEAT: A low-quality humus in which the nitrogen is completely lost through anaerobic fermentation.

PESTICIDE: A chemical used to control any turfgrass pest, such as weeds, insects, and diseases.

pH: An abbreviation for potential hydrogen, used chemically to express the hydrogen ion concentration of a solution. More simply, pH is a scale from 1 to 14, used to denote the relative intensity of acidity or alkalinity. A neutral solution or soil, has a pH of 7.0. Values below 7.0 denote more acid conditions, and those above 7.0 more alkaline conditions.

PHOSPHATE: The fertilizer oxide form of phosphorous (P_2O_5).

PHOSPHORIC ACID: 0-52-0 to 0-55-0

(H_3PO_4) An inorganic acid used in the manufacture of concentrated calcium phosphates and ammonium phosphates and sometimes for direct application through irrigation water.

PHYTOPHTHORA: Latin name for a genus of fungi that causes plant disease, generally a root and crown-rot pathogen.

PHOTOSYNTHESIS: Nature's process of manufacturing carbohydrates from carbon dioxide (CO_2) and water (H_2O) with the use of light energy and green plant pigment called chlorophyll.

PLANT METABOLISM: Those functions of a plant that use energy stored in sugars and carbohydrates to enable the plant to grow and reproduce.

PLUGGING: Establishing a turfgrass using plugs of sod.

POLLEN: A mass of microspores in a seed plant. Looks like a fine dust.

POLYSACCHARIDES: Carbohydrates (complex sugars) of high molecular weight including starch and cellulose.

POTASH: A term used to denote the potassium oxide (K_2O) equivalent of materials containing potassium.

POTASSIUM CHLORIDE: 0-60-0 (KCl) Muriate of potash.

POTASSIUM MAGNESIUM SULFATE ($2MgSO_4K_2SO_4$) Also called sul-po-mag and langbeinite. From natural salt deposits primarily in New Mexico and some European countries. Organic source of K, Mg, and S.

POTASSIUM SULFATE: (K_2SO_4) A solid material with a K_2O equivalent of 45%-52%. Also called sulfate of potash.

PROTEINS: The active, amino acid components of a growing plant. Proteins carry out the bodily activities of the plant, using the energy from sugars and carbohydrates.

PYRETHRUM: Natural insecticide made from the powder of the crushed painted daisy, *Chrysanthemum coccineum*.

QUICKLIME: Burned lime, roasted to drive out carbon dioxide and increase the solubility.

REEL MOWER: A mower that cuts grass by means of a reel guiding the leaves against the cutting edge of the bedknife.

RENOVATION: Improving the vigor of a low-quality soil.

RHIZOBIA: A group of bacteria that penetrates the roots of legumes, extracting carbohydrates from the plant, and capable of fixing atmospheric nitrogen.

RHIZOME: A below-ground stem capable of producing a new plant.

RHIZOSHERE: The soil area immediately adjacent to the root hairs of plants.

ROCK POWDERS: Naturally occurring materials with fertilizing value. The most common rock powders are limestone, rock phosphate, granite dust, greensand, langbeinite (sulfate of potash magnesia), and basalt.

ROOT NODULES: Nodules attached to the roots of legumes and certain nonlegumes. These nodules contain nitrogen-fixing bacteria or nematodes.

ROTARY MOWER: A mower that cuts grass with a high-speed blade that runs parallel to the soil surface.

ROTENONE: Natural insecticide made from the extract of a certain plant root.

SABADILLA: Natural insecticide made from the extract of a tropical lily.

SALT INDEX: The relation of solubilities of chemical compounds. Most nitrogen and potash compounds have a high index, and phosphate compounds have a low index. When applied too close to seed or on foliage, the ones with high indexes can cause plants to wilt or die.

SCALD: Grass that dies under "standing water."

SCALPING: The excessive removal of leaves during mowing, leaving mostly stems.

SEAWEED: Saltwater plants used for fertilizer.

SECONDARY ELEMENTS: The secondary plant food elements as traditionally defined are calcium, magnesium, and sulfur.

SLAG: A byproduct of steel, containing lime, phosphate, and small amounts of other plant food elements such as sulfur, manganese, and iron.

SOAP: A cleansing and emulsifying agent made by action of alkali on fat or fatty acids.

SOD: Plugs, squares, or strips of turf still connected to soil.

SOFT ROCK PHOSPHATE: Colloidal rock phosphate. A by-product of rock phosphate mining.

SOIL: An ecological system consisting of inorganic minerals, organic matter, and living organisms.

SOIL pH: The pH of the water in soil. It controls the availability of phosphorous and trace elements and the diversity of soil organisms. The soil pH for most soils is in the range 5.0 to 9.0, with 7.0 being neutral.

SOIL STRUCTURE: The distribution and size of aggregates in the soil. A good soil structure contains aggregates of widely varying size.

SPRIGGING: Establishing a lawn using sprigs or stolons.

STOLON: An above-ground stem capable of growing a new plant.

STRAW: The above-ground vegetative growth of a plant, usually a small grain or annual legume.

SUGAR: The direct product of photosynthesis. Sugars store the energy absorbed from the sun in the plant leaves.

SULFATE OF POTASH-MAGNESIA: ($2MgSO_4 \bullet K_2SO_4$) A naturally occurring solid material, also called langbeinite, found in salt deposits primarily in New Mexico and in several European countries. The commercial product usually has a K_2O equivalent of about 21%, and contains 53% magnesium sulfate and not more than $2^1/2$% chlorine. It is used in fertilizer as a source of both potash and magnesium.

SULFUR: Normally referred to as a secondary element. It is actually a primary nutrient and is critical in the synthesis of proteins.

SUL-PO-MAG: Mined material consisting of sulfur, potassium, and magnesium. (See sulfate of potash-magnesia).

SUPERPHOSPHATE: The first manufactured phosphorous fertilizer, prepared originally by dissolving bones in sulfuric acid. 0-18-0 to 0-20-0.

SUPERPHOSPHORIC ACID: 0-67-0 to 0-76-0.

TANKAGE: Process tankage is made from leather scrap, wool, and other inert nitrogenous materials by steaming under pressure with or without addition of acid. This treatment increases the availability of the nitrogen to plants.

THATCH: A layer of organic matter that develops between the soil and the base of the plant.

TOP-DRESSING: Spreading a thin layer of soil on the lawn to smooth the surface.

TRANSITION ZONE: An east-west zone through the middle of the U. S. between the northern area, growing cold-season turfgrasses, and the southern area, growing warm-season turfgrasses.

TRIPLE SUPERPHOSPHATE: Rock phosphate dissolved in phosphoric acid.

UREA: 45-0-0 - $CO(NH_2)_2$ A solid synthetic organic material containing approximately 45% nitrogen.

UREA-FORM: Synthetic fertilizer (38-0-0).

VERTICAL MOWING: The use of mechanical device that has vertically rotating blades for thatch control.

VOLATILIZATION: The process of liquid becoming a gas.

WARM-SEASON TURFGRASS: Those turfgrasses used primarily in the southern United States, such as bermudagrass, St. Augustinegrass, zoysiagrass, centipedegrass, and buffalograss.

WILT: The discoloration and folding of leaves caused by either excessively dry or excessively wet conditions.

ZINC SULFATE: $(ZNSO_4 \cdot 7H_2O)$ White vitriol, a solid material used as a source of zinc.

INDEX

INDEX